GREAT AMERICAN

FOR
JAMES BEARD
AND JULIA CHILD,
WHO LIT THE LAMP
AND SHOWED US
THE WAY

COOKING SCHOOLS

GREAT AMERICAN COOKING SCHOOLS

American Food & California Wine
Bountiful Bread: Basics to Brioches
Christmas Feasts from History
Romantic & Classic Cakes
Cooking of the South
Dim Sum & Chinese One-Dish Meals
Fine Fresh Food—Fast
Fresh Garden Vegetables
Ice Cream & Ices
Omelettes & Soufflés
Pasta! Cooking It, Loving It
Quiche & Pâté
Soups & Salads

Cooking of the South

NATHALIE DUPREE

ILLUSTRATED BY WENDY MANSFIELD

IRENA CHALMERS COOKBOOKS, INC. • NEW YORK

IRENA CHALMERS COOKBOOKS, INC.

PUBLISHER
Irena Chalmers

Sales and Marketing Director
Diane J. Kidd

Managing Editor
Jean Atcheson

Series Design
Helene Berinsky

Cover Design
Milton Glaser
Karen Skelton, *Associate Designer*

Cover Photography
Matthew Klein

Editor for this book
Richard Atcheson

Typesetting
Acu-Type, Inc., Clinton, CT

Printing
Lucas Litho, Inc., Baltimore, MD

Editorial Offices
23 East 92nd Street
New York, NY 10028
(212) 289-3105

Sales Offices
P.O. Box 322
Brown Summit, NC 27214
(800) 334-8128

ISBN   0-941034-11-9
© 1982 by Nathalie Dupree. All rights reserved.
Printed and published in the United States of America
by Irena Chalmers Cookbooks, Inc.
LIBRARY OF CONGRESS
CATALOG CARD NO.: 81-70443
  Dupree, Nathalie
    Cooking of the South

Greensboro, NC: Chalmers, Irena Cookbooks, Inc.
84 p.
8110   811007

E D C B A 6 5 4 3 2   695/12

Contents

Introduction

When I'm really hungry I want Southern food, because I know it will fill me up.

The hunger I'm talking about is the kind you feel as a child when you go to church without any breakfast, and halfway through church all you can think about is getting home to dinner. Once you get home, there's at least another half hour of waiting for the chicken to be fried and the table set.

Even if the preacher's there, everyone is a little testy, just anticipating. Of course if the preacher is there, you try to think of ways to divert him from your favorite piece of chicken. The preacher always gets first choice, which means that the little kids wind up with the wings, unless the preacher is smarter than the kids and realizes that the wings taste best.

If you do get skimped on the chicken, there will still be gravy and butter beans and turnip greens and green beans and a few slices of salty ham fried nearly hard, and biscuits to put the gravy on, and tomato conserve to put over the green beans or the butter beans or even the rice. And there will be plenty of iced tea, with the glasses sweating on the white tablecloth; and rich desserts—pecan tassies, coconut cake or cobbler.

After dinner, while the ceiling fan turns, some of the family will nap away the shank of the day on the sofa and in their easy chairs. What food is left will still be on the table, covered with a snowy-white cloth or bedsheet to ward off the flies, ready for more eating at Sunday-night supper.

I remember so well how hungry I'd get, years later, living in London while studying at the Cordon Bleu, where we would eat so elegantly. Sometimes I would wake up just wishing for some Southern green beans with tomato conserve.

Southern cooking is not one thing for rich people and another for poor people. It has its roots in war-torn soil. In the couple of hundred years during which our ways of cooking evolved, a calamitous war was fought and lost on the land; and then the Great Depression deepened the poverty in a region without much industry. Of course there were always pockets of wealth, and of course there are many proud and well-off city Southerners. But true Southern cooking has its foundations in the country kitchen. It is characterized by the gracious willingness to share a meal with strangers as well as loved ones, which is something you will find wherever people have known hard times.

Turnips and collards and peas and beans grow well in poor soil—better, it seems, than in soil that has been fertilized. Pigs are cheap to raise if you let them forage for themselves until it's time to fatten them up for the winter. If you put up tomatoes and peppers and dry some peas, and flavor your peas and collards with fat from the pig you killed for the winter, you can get by. In the South they say, "If you have black-eyed peas on New Year's Day, you'll have plenty of change during the year." But, "With collard greens or turnip greens you'll have greenbacks all year long." That's Southern economics.

Southerners don't always agree on the way to cook something, because so much of the tradition is passed down from generation to generation by doing and showing, and is rarely written down. There are hundreds of recipes for barbecue and fried chicken and you'll find no two alike. Celeste Dupree, who looked over these recipes before they were sent to the publisher, was worried because they didn't specify frying the chicken in bacon drippings, which is what her mother's recipes call for. (And it's a wonderful way to do it, by the way.) I did follow her advice on my stewed tomato conserve recipe, adding more cider vinegar, which made it even better than it was before.

I started Rich's Cooking School at the famous department store in Atlanta after I'd been back in Georgia for a few years running a French restaurant I opened up across from the Tri-County Cattle Auction Barn out at Hub Junction. That's where Kate Almand, from Social Circle, Georgia, came into my life. She went to work with me in the restaurant, helping to make bread and learning to beat egg whites by hand in a copper bowl. When I was tired of my own French cooking, she and her friend Grace would take time out to cook their Southern food for me.

Kate was born in rural Georgia. There were 13 children in the family, and as a child she always helped with the cooking. Her way is to use fresh local ingredients, and sometimes all of it she has raised herself—vegetables, hogs and chickens. I believe she was born with a biscuit bowl in her hands as other people are born with silver spoons in their mouths. I'd rather have her gift for baking biscuits than any number of silver spoons.

When I started the cooking school, Kate joined me at Rich's, and she's still there every day,

mothering the students—hundreds of them—and happily showing them how to make biscuits her way, on request.

In a way, this is Kate's book as much as mine. For years we've been comparing recipes and our different ways of doing things, and here we have come up with recipes that relate to our land, and will, we hope, suit many people (you can't suit everyone).

These days famous cooks and chefs often drop by the cooking school to sample Kate's cooking, but it doesn't surprise her. She has grown grandchildren now, and her children and grandchildren all still come to dinner with Kate and her husband, David, whenever they can. When Bert Greene makes a detour to taste her biscuits on his way from New York to Florida, she just wishes he'd get to Atlanta more often. She's cooked for Julia Child and debated chicken-frying with Craig Claiborne. She knows God loves them, and they don't faze *her* because God loves everyone the same. And she likes their cooking too.

Many of the old recipes are lost, to my regret. I've gone into the kitchens of family and friends from Maryland and Virginia to Mississippi and Louisiana, taking notes as they cook, trying to find ways to describe a kind of cooking that is second nature and not easily put into words. Some of my favorite food memories from my Virginia childhood have proved to be unduplicatable. Was it really just bread soaked in sweet milk and sprinkled with sugar that made me get over my grief one day as a child? David Dupree's grandmother's caramel cake recipe still eludes me, and I've had to omit it, reluctantly, along with the famous Southern Lane Cakes and White Lily Cakes, which simply can't be duplicated using Northern flour.

A large part of the base of our cuisine is from other traditions—English, French, Moravian, African, Spanish, even West Indian. I've tried to weed out the obviously borrowed carry-ons (like Charlotte Russe and Lasagna) often cooked by today's Southern cooks, but have left alone many of the derived dishes (Sally Lunns, for instance) that are so pervasive that they are considered to be Southern. Some Southern areas that have developed their own cuisines—Texas/New Mexico; New Orleans, Creole and Cajun—I've left out because they deserve books in their own right. However, some elements that have wandered from those places into other parts of the South, like the spicy baked shrimp from New Orleans, will be found here. Also, I've added things that adapt themselves so well to the South that they should have been created down here, long ago, so well suited are they to our modern styles of entertaining. These include Turnip Gratinée, Green Beans and Potatoes Piquant, Zucchini Soup, and Sausage and Apple Quiche.

While I owe so much to Kate, we both owe Martha Summerour and Sarah Rhodes a great deal too. The two of them always insisted that the foods around us were as important as the French dishes we were teaching, and that the recipes for them needed to be recorded. Martha taught our first Southern cooking classes, and helped start the writing down of recipes.

I also need to thank Elise Griffin, who so patiently made the recipes into a cohesive whole, and I want to thank Fred Brown, publisher and editor of *Brown's Guide to Georgia*, for giving me permission to reprint some of the recipes he inspired. And, of course, I am very grateful to Kay Calvert for typing the recipes, and to Rich's for the Cooking School itself, and to the assistants and teachers there for their constant help.

What We Eat

The most important elements of Southern cooking are fats and frying, peas and beans, the vegetables of the region, Southern flour, sweet milk and buttermilk, and of course chicken.

Pork fat is the standard ingredient used in Southern cooking, to flavor and preserve foods. It can be fresh or cured. When the fat comes from the back of the animal it is called fatback, and is only fat. When it is streaked with meat, like bacon (but cured differently), it is called streak-of-lean or streak-o'-lean. When you can't find fatback, any salt pork will do. When you can't find streak-o'-lean, use bacon. Bacon drippings melted, and butter and shortening, melted, are used as well as lard, which is also melted.

The South isn't always particular about what it calls a bean and what it calls a pea; peas and beans are both legumes. Black-eyed peas are really beans. Both are a necessary part of the South's cooking, and furnish important protein. They are usually cooked a very long time, whether fresh or dried, the dried ones having been soaked in water first. Coupled with rice, they form a complete protein. With the addition of pork or pork fat, they make an even more substantial meal.

Southern vegetables traditionally are cooked for a long time. My theory is that they were put on the back of the stove over low heat for the whole day so that no one would have to stay in the hot kitchen to watch them, since everyone needed to be busy elsewhere. Vegetables could be made early in the day, then allowed to stand, and then be reheated for the noon meal. There are many good reasons why vegetables shouldn't be cooked hours and hours — nutritionists say that important vitamins are lost, and my mother-in-law says that turnip greens cooked too long make you sick. But most Southerners couldn't care less and still cook anything green as long as they please.

Southern flour is low in gluten (8 or 9 percent). It makes wonderful pies, and biscuits that are unbelievably light. When you use Northern flours (which have a much higher gluten content) with recipes in this book, try using some cake flour in place of the regular bleached or unbleached flour. The difference in flours is quite radical. The purest Southern flour is White Lily, but there are many others, including Martha White. Self-rising flour can be made by adding 1½ teaspoons baking powder and ½ teaspoon salt to each cup of plain flour.

The term "sweet milk" means regular milk, whether homogenized or pasteurized. Buttermilk, which has a more acid flavor, is what is left when the milk has been clabbered and churned to make butter.

It's obvious that the reason we have a lot of fried foods in the South is that lard is cheap.

When fat is plentiful, frying is economical. It is cheaper than heating up an oven, and puts flesh on your bones to keep you warm in the winter.

In Southern cooking, chickens are usually fried. Chicken recipes here, unless stated otherwise, call for 2½-pound chickens.

What We Drink

Wines are not usually served at a typical Southern table. In the last 10 years, we have seen an upsurge in wine-drinking, but it is still unusual in Southern homes to be offered wine with a meal. First of all, the South still has traces of the Bible belt around its middle. Many people in small towns or cities don't drink at all, and for those that do, it's probably bourbon or beer. Cola is popular, and the other standby is iced tea, or "sweet ice tea." When I do want to serve wine with a Southern meal, I prefer a light white wine, except for pork and barbecues; Spanish and Italian red wines are good with these.

Recipes

APPETIZERS

When I was growing up, everything in a Southern meal was put on the table at the same time. If you were lucky, there would be some toasted pecans and maybe some peanuts put out in the living room before dinner—or even some cheese straws. We're a land of folks who drop by when they see the lights on in a neighbor's house, especially on Sunday and on Wednesday nights after church. And the invitation, earnestly proffered, to "come see us," is a constant refrain. Any self-respecting household has cheese straws in the freezer or in an airtight tin, and something sweet under the cake dome on the sideboard. So the things commonly thought of elsewhere as appetizers may be offered in the South in many situations—not only just to whet the appetite before a meal, but just as often as the first course of a sit-down formal meal when there is someone hired to serve. You might find these things at ladies' tea parties, or at bridge parties, or offered with coffee, iced or hot tea, or drinks (mainly "co'cola") any time during the day. Cheese straws are also brought to the cities by grandmothers who live in the country— made by grandmother herself, or by one of the legion of small-town caterers who cook in their home kitchens for others; an important Southern cottage industry.

Toasted Pecans

Makes 1 quart

These are regulars at every Atlanta cocktail party. Variations may include curry powder or other spices, but for those who love pecans, this is the best way.

1 quart fine quality pecan halves
8 tablespoons butter
Salt

Preheat the oven to 250 degrees. Put the pecans on a large baking sheet and dot them with butter. Bake for 1 hour, stirring occasionally. Remove them from the oven and salt them while they are hot. Store in a tightly covered container.

Cheese Straws

Makes 50 to 60

1 pound sharp New York cheddar, grated
16 tablespoons butter
3¼ - 3½ cups flour
1 tablespoon salt
Red pepper to taste

Preheat the oven to 375 degrees. Cream the cheese and butter together. Add the rest of the ingredients. Put in a cookie press with a cheese straw blade. Bake for 10 to 15 minutes. Do not brown.

Sausage and Apple Quiche

Serves 4

Cut this quiche into small pieces as an appetizer for a crowd, or into wedges for a luncheon or light supper. The fall is a perfect time for this, with the apples from our Virginia, North Carolina or Georgia mountains and our rural sausage.

½ pound hot sausage (bulk style)
2 medium-size apples, peeled, cored and sliced
9-inch pie crust, baked (see page 74)
¾ cup heavy cream
2 eggs

Preheat the oven to 375 degrees.

Brown the sausage in a skillet over medium heat. Add the apple slices and cook until barely tender. Place in the baked pastry. Mix the liquid ingredients together and pour over the sausage mixture, being careful not to overfill. Bake 20 to 25 minutes or until firm in the center.

NOTE: Frozen pie shells make this dish quick to prepare.

Potted Pork

This is wonderful for excess pork of any kind, and we have a lot of it in Georgia. This dish refrigerates for a long time when covered with the preserving fat, and it freezes well.

½ pound salt fatback, trimmed of rind and rinsed well
2 pounds pork, loin or spare ribs, weighed after bone is removed
1 cup cold water
Salt and freshly ground pepper to taste
5 garlic cloves, finely chopped
1 pinch allspice
½ teaspoon sage

Preheat the oven to 300 degrees.

Cut the salt fatback into fine dice (⅛ inch by ¼ inch). Place in a 5-quart ovenproof casserole and render for half an hour. Cut the pork into strips about 1 inch long and ½ inch thick or chop roughly in a food processor. When fat is liquid but not brown, add the pork, 1 cup of cold water and the salt and pepper. The fat and liquid should cover the meat; add additional thin slices of fatback if it does not. Cover the casserole and place it in a baking pan which is half filled with water. Put it in the oven. Cook for 45 minutes, checking occasionally to see that there is still water in the pan. The meat should be very soft and still covered with clear liquid fat. It should not be brown or fried-looking. Take a large sieve and a mixing bowl and drain the meat, saving the fat.

Using 2 forks, pull and tease the meat to separate the fibers. As you work, transfer the loose meat to another bowl, and add a few tablespoons of the reserved liquid fat to the shredded meat. Add salt, pepper, garlic, allspice and sage. Transfer to sterile (straight from the dishwasher) storage jars or pots; fill well below the tops. Do not pack down too tightly. Allow to cool, then cover with either hot liquid fat or plastic film. Before serving, allow it to come to room temperature. Serve with crusty bread and pickles.

Delicious Crisp-Fried Salt Pork

I've never had anything quite like this in other cuisines. Called "Tennessee Chicken" by Kate, this fried pork fat has a puffy exterior like a potato chip and a soft, melted interior. It is crispy and crunchy.

2 teaspoons lard or shortening
¾ pound fatback (salt pork), thinly sliced
½ cup buttermilk
½-¾ cup flour

Heat the shortening in an iron skillet. Dip each slice of fatback into buttermilk, dust in flour and add to hot shortening. Fry until golden brown. (The pan will probably only hold half the slices at a time.) Turn once. Drain on paper towel.

Buffet Chicken Drumettes

This is a perfect dish for cocktail buffets, picnics or as a snack with which to greet travelers. It freezes well.

24 drumettes (first joint of chicken wing)
Juice of 4 lemons
Juice of 2 limes
Salt to taste
Freshly ground pepper
2 teaspoons ground ginger
1 garlic clove, finely chopped
3 tablespoons chopped parsley
1 tablespoon chopped fresh tarragon or 1½ teaspoons dried
3 tablespoons chopped fresh dill weed or 1 tablespoon dried
Hungarian paprika, to taste
½ cup butter, melted

Preheat the oven to 375 degrees.

Put the chicken pieces in pans lined with buttered aluminum foil. Mix the fruit juices and sprinkle half over the chicken. Mix the herbs and spices together and sprinkle them over the chicken. Dribble melted butter over all. Cover loosely with foil and bake for 25 minutes. Remove the foil and bake 20 minutes longer.

Remove the chicken from the pan and pour the remaining juices over. Serve hot or cold. This dish may be made 1 to 2 days ahead.

Grits Roulade

This recipe was invented by David Dupree and me in the wee hours of the morning. It was used for a Rich's store promotion and grits contest just before Jimmy Carter was elected President.

ROULADE:

⅓ cup plain yogurt
⅔ cup milk
½ cup instant grits
⅔ cup grated cheddar cheese or
   ⅓ cup Swiss and ⅓ cup Parmesan
   cheeses, mixed
4 egg yolks
Salt and pepper to taste
6 egg whites

FILLING:

2 cups fresh mushrooms, sliced
5 tablespoons butter
Ham, optional (½ cup, sliced or
   chopped)
4½ tablespoons flour
3 cups milk

Preheat the oven to 350 degrees.

Oil a 10½-by-15½-inch jelly-roll pan, then oil wax paper and line the pan.

Heat the yogurt and milk to boiling (the mixture will look curdled), then add the instant grits and cook by the package directions. Add the cheese and egg yolks, one at a time, then salt and pepper. Beat the egg whites until they stand in firm peaks. Fold in a spoonful of the egg whites to soften the grits mixture. Then fold the whole mixture into the rest of the whites. Do not overfold. When all the egg whites are folded in, spread the entire mixture into the jelly-roll pan. Smooth the top. Bake for 20 to 25 minutes. (The top should spring back lightly when it is touched and a toothpick inserted into it should come out clean. Do not overcook or it will crack.) When done, remove it from the oven and turn the pan upside down onto another piece of wax paper. Remove the pan and strip the wax paper from the roulade.

To make the filling: Cook the mushrooms lightly in a small skillet with 1 tablespoon of the butter until they are tender. Add more butter if needed. Add ham, if you want it, and set aside. Melt the remaining 4 tablespoons of butter in a pan and add the flour. Stir in the milk and cook until thickened. Add the mushroom mixture and blend thoroughly.

Spread the mushroom filling over the grits and roll up like a jelly roll, beginning from the long side.

NOTE: This dish may be made a day ahead and reheated for 10 minutes in a 350-degree oven.

Onion Flowers with Pecans

Serves 4

There is a special onion grown in Vidalia, Georgia and a bit of the area surrounding Vidalia. It's said that the onions are so sweet you can eat them out of your hand, as you would an apple. If you can get Vidalia onions, do!

4 large sweet onions
Salt to taste
4 teaspoons red wine vinegar
4-6 tablespoons melted butter
2-3 tablespoons chopped pecans or
   8-12 pecan halves
Freshly ground pepper
Chopped parsley

Make this the day before you serve it.

Preheat the oven to 350 degrees.

Peel the onions, leaving the roots trimmed but intact. Cut in ¼-inch slices from stem to root, but don't cut through the root end. (A needle or skewer stuck through the root will prevent this.) Turn each onion at right angles and cut again so that when you stand it on its root end, it will form a chrysanthemum design. For another style, cut nearly through the root, turn, and cut again, as you would with pie wedges, at 45-degree angles. Don't worry about any loose onion sections in the middle.

Oil a baking dish lightly. Salt the onions and place them on their root ends in the baking dish. Sprinkle vinegar over each onion and dribble butter over them until they are well coated and there is extra fat in the pan for basting. Cover lightly with foil and bake for 1 to 1½ hours, basting several times. Add a few chopped pecans to the center of each onion and continue baking another ½ hour.

Remove from the oven, season with salt and pepper and sprinkle with chopped parsley. Serve hot or at room temperature. They may also be refrigerated and served cold.

Wilted Cucumbers

Despite its name, this is a very refreshing dish that works well as either a salad or a vegetable. It adds a cool touch to any buffet.

2 small cucumbers, peeled
Salt
¼ cup sour cream
1 tablespoon lemon juice or vinegar
1 teaspoon sugar, or to taste
Tomato cups (optional) or sliced
**   tomatoes**

Slice the cucumbers very thin and layer them in a dish, sprinkling each layer with salt. Place plastic wrap directly on the cucumbers and weight them with a heavy pan. Let stand for about 2 hours.

Pour off the water, rinse the cucumbers in a colander with cold water, and squeeze them in a tea towel until they are dry. Combine the sour cream, lemon juice or vinegar and sugar, and toss with the cucumbers. Serve alone, in tomato cups, or surrounded by sliced tomatoes.

To make Tomato Cups: Cut a slice off the stem end of each tomato. Carefully remove the seeds with a teaspoon. Sprinkle with salt, turn upside down and allow to drain.

Tomato Aspic

Aspic is as typically Southern as iced tea. It is seen whenever a "special time" is involved for "old South" parties. This is a better-flavored and more interesting aspic than you will get from many other recipes.

1-pound can tomatoes
1 small onion, finely chopped
4 cloves
1 teaspoon fresh or dried basil
1 bay leaf
2 tablespoons gelatin
1 cup cold water
Juice of 3 lemons
Salt to taste
1 tablespoon sugar, or to taste
½ cup sliced ripe olives (optional)

Combine the tomatoes, onion, cloves, basil and bay leaf in a small saucepan. Simmer for 20 minutes. Strain and reserve the hot tomato juice.

In another small saucepan, combine the gelatin with cold water and allow it to soften. Place over low heat and let the gelatin dissolve. Stir it into the tomato juice. Add lemon juice, salt, sugar and olives if desired.

Grease a 3-cup mold with salad oil. Pour the gelatin mixture into the prepared mold and chill. Unmold and serve on lettuce with mayonnaise on the side.

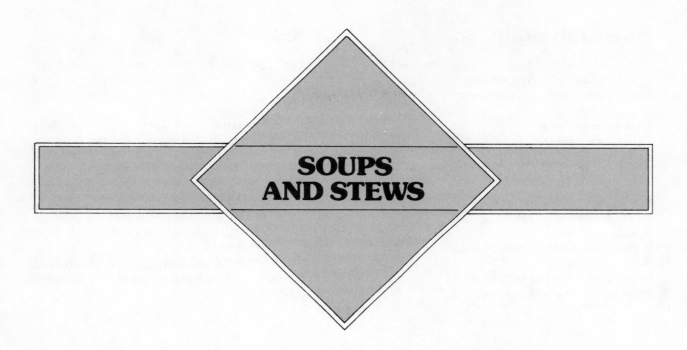

SOUPS AND STEWS

Soups are not just "starters" for a meal—often, in fact, they are the whole meal. Our soups and stews divide themselves pretty easily. They are made in the flash of an eye—like oyster stew and she-crab soup—or they take a long time to fix and—like Brunswick stew and pine-forest stew—they taste better the longer they take. There's a similar difference in how they age. Oyster stew should be eaten right away, and never rewarmed if it can be avoided. Brunswick stew, on the other hand, gets better and better the more it is reheated. Cucumber soup and zucchini soup are new concepts in the South, but they're growing in popularity because both vegetables are plentiful and have a long growing season in Southern climes. Frequently these soups are served out in cups, in the living room before dinner, unless there is some help in the kitchen to serve courses in the dining room.

You can hear stories told about all kinds of Southern dishes, and many of them seem to be pretty tall stories indeed. The one told about Brunswick stew is this: It seems that, long ago, the Earl of Brunswick came visiting the Southern colonies and was served a lavish, overdone meal in a fancy private home. Supposedly, he pushed himself away from the laden table and declared that he wanted to eat some honest food, food that the "peasants" were eating. His fancy hosts went and scared up some local folks, and they were found to be eating a stew which the Earl sampled and said was one of the best things he ever put in his mouth. Everyone was tickled to death and they called that dish Brunswick stew ever afterward and to this day.

She-Crab Soup

This is a traditional favorite along the coast around Savannah and Charleston. It is garnished with the eggs of the crab, so it is a seasonal recipe. It can be made with "boy-crabs," and with the crumbled yolks of hard-cooked eggs as a substitute for the eggs of the crab.

1 tablespoon butter
2 teaspoons flour
1 quart milk
2 cups white crab meat with eggs
Salt
Freshly ground white pepper
A few drops onion juice
⅛ teaspoon mace
½ teaspoon Worcestershire sauce
¼ cup dry sherry
½ cup heavy cream, whipped
Paprika or chopped parsley

Melt the butter, add the flour, and stir until smooth. Add the milk and bring it to a boil, stirring constantly. Remove from heat, cool for a few minutes, and add the crab meat, eggs, salt, pepper, onion juice, mace and Worcestershire sauce. Cook slowly for 20 minutes. Do not boil or heat over 180 degrees. Use a double boiler if necessary.

To serve, place 1 tablespoon of sherry in each soup bowl, ladle the soup in and top with whipped cream. Sprinkle with paprika or finely chopped parsley.

NOTE: If you are unable to obtain crab eggs, crumble bits of the yolks of two hard-cooked eggs in the bottom of each soup bowl just before serving.

Iced Cucumber Soup

This cold soup can be made in great batches and kept for several days in the refrigerator. In this case, don't add the cucumbers ahead of time because they water down the soup. The shrimp should be fresh. Be sure to taste the cucumber before you make the soup since it often happens that cucumbers that did not have enough rain while growing are bitter.

2-3 cucumbers, peeled and diced
¼ cup salt
½ cup tomato juice
½ cup chicken stock, fresh or canned
2½ cups plain yogurt
½ cup heavy cream
2 garlic cloves, finely chopped
1 hard-cooked egg, grated
3 ounces small shrimp, cooked,
   peeled and chopped
Fresh mint, finely chopped
   (optional)

Put the diced cucumbers in a colander, sprinkle them with the salt and allow to drain for 30 minutes. Rinse well, pat dry, and set aside.

Meanwhile, combine the tomato juice, chicken stock, yogurt, cream, garlic and egg. Chill. Add the cucumbers and shrimp. Garnish with chopped mint if you wish.

Zucchini Soup

Zucchini didn't make a mark on the South until the last 10 years. Now, however, they are everywhere, because they proliferate here.

4 small zucchini, thinly sliced
¼ cup salt
3 tablespoons butter
2 onions, finely chopped
1 garlic clove, finely chopped
3½ cups chicken stock, fresh or canned
1-2 tablespoons mixed fresh herbs, finely chopped (parsley, chives, oregano, basil), or 1 teaspoon dried herbs
1 teaspoon lemon juice
⅓ cup heavy cream
Freshly ground black pepper to taste
1 cup sour cream

Salt the zucchini and let stand for half an hour. Heat the butter. Add the onion and the garlic and cook in a pan over low heat for 5 minutes, covered with wax paper. Rinse and dry the zucchini very well. Add them to the skillet, reserving a few for garnish, and continue cooking over low heat for 5 minutes. Add the chicken stock and let the soup simmer for 15 minutes. Then strain the solids and reserve the liquid.

Puree the solids, in batches, in a food processor or blender, adding liquid as needed to make the puree. Add the herbs, lemon juice, cream, and as much more liquid as will make the desired consistency. Blend to mix.

Season with salt and pepper and chill the soup until serving time. Garnish with sour cream and few slices of the zucchini. You can also serve this soup hot if you prefer.

Soup of Small Birds

This is an adaptation of a recipe in "Pines and Plantations," a book of native recipes from Thomasville, Georgia. It is recommended as a way of serving game birds when you don't have enough to roast.

3 or more pounds squab, guinea hen, quail, and/or duck
⅓ cup butter and oil, combined
1 tablespoon brown sugar
½ cup chopped onions
½ cup chopped carrots
1 teaspoon marjoram
1 teaspoon thyme
1 cup red wine
6 or more cups chicken broth or stock, heated
1 cup heavy cream, scalded
2 egg yolks
1 jigger Cognac
Chopped parsley
Croutons, fried in butter

Clean and dry the birds. Cook them in the butter and oil until they are golden all over. You can split them in half so that the liquid added later will cover them more easily. When they are browned, put them in a large soup kettle. Add the brown sugar, onions, carrots, herbs, wine and hot broth. Cover; bring to a simmer and skim. Cover again and cook gently for 1 hour. Strain the mixture, saving the broth.

Remove all the meat from the bones and cut 2 cups of it into cubes; puree the rest with the reserved broth. If it is too thick, add a little more broth. Put the diced meat in the soup.

When ready to serve, reheat the soup gradually. Mix the scalded cream with the egg yolks and whisk into the soup. Reheat, but do not boil. Add the Cognac. Ladle into individual bowls and sprinkle the top of each with chopped parsley. Pass the crisp croutons on the side.

Cream of Carrot Soup

This is a delicious way to serve one of the most useful of root vegetables.

3 tablespoons butter
5-6 carrots, peeled and thinly sliced
1 onion, thinly sliced
4 cups chicken stock (or canned broth)
1½ tablespoons sugar (or to taste)
Freshly ground pepper to taste
½ clove garlic, crushed with salt
¾ cup heavy cream
¼ cup cooked rice

Melt 2 tablespoons of the butter in a large saucepan; add the carrots and onion. Stir in the stock, cover and simmer for about 30 minutes, or until the vegetables are very soft. Pour off the liquid and reserve it.

Puree the vegetables, in small batches, in a food processor or blender. Then return both the puree and the liquid to the saucepan. Add the sugar and season to taste with the crushed garlic and freshly ground pepper. Add the cream, bring just to a boil and immediately remove the saucepan from the heat. Whisk in the remaining tablespoon of butter. Garnish with the cooked rice.

NOTE: This soup may be made several days ahead and reheated gently. Be sure not to add the butter until the final heating is complete.

Oyster Stew

Oyster stew stands alone, served with tiny oyster crackers. You need to crumble the crackers quickly just before you dip a spoon into the bowl so that there is a crunch of the cracker, a soft oyster, a little flush of flavor from the tiny bits of green pepper and onion that creep onto the spoon, and finally a rich creamy finish taste of butter and cream and oyster juices. The first spoonful is the best, except for the last. Try it late at night, or on a mean winter Saturday for lunch.

2-4 tablespoons butter
½ teaspoon finely chopped onion
1 clove garlic, finely chopped
¼ cup finely chopped celery
1 tablespoon finely chopped green pepper
1-1½ pints oysters with liquid
1½ cups milk
½ cup heavy cream
½ teaspoon salt
Freshly ground white pepper
2 tablespoons chopped parsley

Melt the butter in a heavy saucepan. Add the onion, garlic, celery and green pepper. Cook until nearly soft. Add the oysters and their liquid, milk, cream, salt and pepper. Heat slowly. Do not boil, or it may curdle. When the liquid is hot and the oysters float, it is done. Add chopped parsley and serve.

Brunswick Stew

Makes 2 gallons

My friend Kate makes her Brunswick stew from one of her own hogs when she can, using the head. (Good Southern cooks know that the cheek and head of the hog give some of the best flavors.) She says, "My family wouldn't eat hog's head just like it is. It has to be disguised, and Brunswick stew is a good way to do it." Kate's Christmas gift of Brunswick stew in one-pint containers will get me through January and February and a bit of March.

4-pound stewing hen
4 pounds beef, ground or boneless roast
4 pounds pork roast, including bones (or hog's head)
4 1-pound cans tomatoes, undrained
1-pound can corn, drained
2 onions, chopped
12-ounce bottle catsup
1 tablespoon cayenne pepper or less
Salt and pepper to taste

Put the meat and poultry, still on the bones, into a large kettle or Dutch oven. Cover with water. Cook over medium heat until all the meat comes off the bone, adding water if needed. Drain and save the liquid. Remove the meat from the bones and run it through a meat grinder or chop it in a food processor. Run the tomatoes, corn and onions through the grinder or chop them in a food processor. Put the meat and poultry, tomatoes, corn, onions and catsup into a large pot. Add the cayenne, salt, pepper and enough of the reserved liquid to make a stew-like consistency. Cook 30 minutes over low heat to combine the flavors. Serve hot. The stew may be frozen when cool.

Pine-Forest Stew

Serves 6 to 8

My friend Conrad Zimmerman from Charleston is a hunter, and he believes that what he eats when he is hunting is as important as what he eats when he's at home. He named this stew after his favorite camping spot. He says you fix it on those special nights hunters know, under trees 100 feet high, with pine straw a foot deep on the ground and not a whisper of sound.

½-1 pound bacon
Flour
Salt
Garlic powder
Fresh-killed game
Pepper
8 stalks celery cut in 2-inch lengths
6 carrots cut in 2-inch lengths
6 potatoes, peeled and quartered
1-pound can tomatoes
1 bay leaf
5 teaspoons thyme
French bread
Fifth of red wine

Place a black iron pot over the fire. Chop up the bacon, add it to the pan and stir until it starts to crinkle. Place the flour, salt, garlic powder and pepper in a paper bag.

Put the meat, whatever you shot—squirrels, quartered rabbits, dove, quail—in a paper bag and shake it up. Put it in the pot, and stir until the game is browned. Add the celery, carrots and potatoes to the pot. Pour in enough water to cover the vegetables and meat. Add the tomatoes, bay leaf, thyme and a palmful of pepper and salt, mixed. Sprinkle in a little more garlic powder. Put a lid on the pot. Hang the pot from a chain or tripod, and simmer 1½ hours while telling stories and drinking the wine. Every once in a while, take a piece of French bread and dip it in the pot for an appetizer. When ready to serve, take a piece of bread, pour stew over it, and throw the bones over your shoulder. You can add a pack of green peas or another vegetable if you want.

VEGETABLES AND RELISHES

The music of the table—the many different themes, colors and textures—comes from the vegetables. There are always more of them on the Southern table than you can possibly eat; each bowl contains more than a whole family would consume at one sitting. So they give a feeling of abundance where, in fact, there might not be any at all, making you able to push yourself away from the table feeling (as you are supposed to, in the South) a little bit too full. The vegetables are reheated, of course, frequently without refrigerating, between times of lunch (we call it dinner) and supper, after resting awhile in their covered china dishes. And then more fresh vegetables are added to the table at the next meal.

We pride ourselves on our garden-fresh vegetables, and even the fanciest homes will have a turnip patch out back, or a place to grow collards. The liquid from the vegetables is called pot-liquor (pot-likker) and is used for dunking cornbread and biscuits. Sometimes the likker is served by itself, when the vegetables are all gone and the liquid has been boiled up a bit to make it heartier. Then it becomes a soup.

Fresh Crowder Peas with Snaps

Serves 6

Peas may be cooked when they are freshly picked or dried. If they are fresh, they are called "green" peas, regardless of the variety. What are known as green peas in many areas of the United States are called "English" peas here. Other peas also have names, such as lady peas, crowder peas, etc. The crowders are divided again into purple hulls, sugar crowders, etc. Fresh peas cook faster than dried. Lady peas are similar to field peas and crowder peas, but they are smaller and more flavorful. They can be found fresh or dried. (Soak at least one hour if dried.)

2½ pounds fresh crowders or lady peas to get 1½ pounds shelled
3 ounces of fatback (salt pork)
4 cups water to cover
1 small red hot pepper (optional)

Shell the peas, and check for worm holes. If you have any pods that are too tiny to shell, leave them whole or snap them in half. Cook these "snaps" with the shelled peas.

Place the peas and snaps in a heavy pan. Slice into the fatback four times but leave it whole with the rind intact. Add 4 cups of water to the peas, snaps and fatback. Add pepper if you wish and cover. Let the mixture come to a boil, then turn it down to simmer. The peas are done when the fat is done, in about an hour.

LADY PEAS

1½ pounds shelled lady peas

Cover with water and simmer gently to prevent bursting. These tiny, tender peas can be seasoned French-style with herbs, garlic and butter, or Southern-style with meat, fatback or butter.

Cabbage

Many people cook cabbage with fatback or salt pork, but this recipe of Kate's is better by far. Dip cornbread into the pot likker.

1 large head of cabbage
1 teaspoon salt
1½ cups water
½ cup butter

Cut the cabbage in quarters and remove the core. Slice each quarter into 6 pieces. Put them in a medium-sized saucepan with water and salt. Cook, uncovered, for 30 minutes. Add butter and cook 15 minutes longer.

Little Limas *(BUTTER BEANS)*

Butter beans are a smaller version of lima beans, with a sweeter, clearer taste than lima beans and much less mealiness. Although many people cook them with "streak-of-lean," Kate cooks them with butter.

4 cups fresh shelled butter beans
8 cups water
¼ cup butter or "streak-of-lean"
Salt
Freshly ground pepper

Place the butter beans in a heavy wide saucepan or deep skillet with twice as much water (8 cups) as beans. Add butter or fat, salt, and fresh pepper to taste. Cook approximately 30 to 45 minutes, stirring only when necessary to prevent browning.

Fried Corn

Fried corn is not really fried, it's stewed in a frying pan. Field corn such as "Silver Queen" or "Truckers' Favorite" grows to a bigger, thicker corn than sweet corn (and, obviously, is not as sweet). Rarely do you see field corn in grocery stores. Field corn makes better fried corn but any kind can be used.

**1 ounce fatback (salt pork) cut into
  4 thin slices
8 ears field or sweet corn
1-2 cups water
6 tablespoons butter
1-1½ teaspoons salt**

Place the fatback slices in a heavy 10-inch iron skillet or heavy non-stick pan.

Using a knife or corn cutter, tip the top of the grains off all around a corn cob; then go back and scrape the remaining corn off the cob. Repeat with the rest of the corn, extracting all "milk" from the cob. (This is done to avoid getting whole kernels.)

When the fatback has rendered 3 to 4 tablespoons of liquid fat, remove the slices, leaving the fat. Add the corn and corn milk to the fat. Add water. If the corn is thick and mature you may need to add more. If young, add less. Stir in the water and bring to a boil, stirring. Add butter and salt. Turn to low and cook, stirring occasionally to prevent sticking. It's done when it is thick and sticky and the corn is tender; about half an hour.

Fried Green Tomatoes

This was a favorite dish of my childhood in Virginia, served with eggs fried sunny side up in the same butter, for lunch or dinner, or even for a midnight snack.

**2-3 green tomatoes
½-⅔ cup flour or corn meal
½ cup butter or oil**

Rinse the tomatoes and slice in half-inch slices. Place the flour or meal on wax paper and coat the tomatoes on one side, then the other. Heat enough fat to cover the bottom of a frying pan or iron skillet. Re-flour the tomatoes and fry 4 to 5 slices at a time until golden brown, then turn. Remove and place on a paper towel while frying the rest. Serve immediately.

Fried Okra

Okra pods should be little, not much bigger than the size of your little finger. When they are any larger, or old, their milky substance dilutes the fat and you wind up with a mess. (It is possible to fry frozen okra, but it doesn't come out as well as fresh-cooked.) Okra should be eaten right away. In fact, it rarely lasts from the skillet to the table because of the snitching that goes on while it cooks.

1 pound okra
½ cup corn meal or ¼ cup corn meal
    and ¼ cup flour, mixed
1 teaspoon salt
1 cup peanut or vegetable oil, or
    melted shortening
Freshly ground pepper

Rinse the okra, remove the caps, and cut the pods in half, or into quarter-inch pieces. Mix the corn meal, flour and salt. Toss the okra with the mixture. Spread the pods out for a few minutes to dry, then toss them in the meal mixture again. Meanwhile, pour the oil halfway up the sides of a heavy skillet or iron frying pan. Heat to sizzling, add the okra and leave enough room to turn the pods. Fry until they are lightly browned, turning only to prevent burning. (Too much turning and tossing will leave a residue of browned meal in the bottom of the pan. If this happens, add more oil and fry the rest of the okra. Then strain the fat and clean the pan with paper towel to eliminate the browned residue.) Add salt and freshly ground pepper while still hot.

Fried Yellow Squash

Serves 8

Many times Southern foods are called fried that really aren't fried at all, but are cooked in a skillet. This dish is served with other country vegetables any time yellow squash is fresh.

1½ pounds yellow squash, sliced
 (4 or 5 individual gourds)
1 cup water
1 small onion, sliced
Salt and freshly ground pepper,
 to taste
3 tablespoons fatback drippings
3 tablespoons butter

Combine the squash, water, onions, salt and freshly ground pepper in a skillet. Bring to a boil and cook, uncovered, until the water evaporates. Add the fatback drippings and butter. Cook slowly for 35 minutes, stirring frequently.

Potatoes and Green Beans Piquant

Serves 8

This is wonderful with home-grown vegetables. If you are using "pole beans," cut them into ½-inch diamonds. This dish is good lukewarm or cold, and may be served as a salad or a vegetable.

1 pound tiny fresh green beans
2 pounds tiny new potatoes
1 cup dressing (see below)

DRESSING:
¾ cup salad or peanut oil
¼ cup white or red wine vinegar
1 teaspoon Dijon mustard
1 small garlic clove, finely chopped
Salt and freshly ground pepper to
 taste
¼ teaspoon sugar
2 tablespoons chopped fresh herbs
 (basil, tarragon, etc.), or
 2 teaspoons dried
Dash of pepper juice or a little
 chopped red hot pepper (optional)

To make the dressing, combine all the ingredients in a quart jar, cover well and shake to blend. Reshake the jar just before using. Add pepper juice or chopped pepper, if desired.

Remove the tips from the beans, but leave them whole; boil them in salted water to cover for 7 to 10 minutes, or until they are still crunchy. Remove from heat, drain, and immediately rinse them with cold water to refresh and retain their color. Meanwhile, cook whole, unpeeled new potatoes in boiling salted water to cover until done (about 20 minutes). Drain. While they are still hot, peel the potatoes quickly and toss them in half of the dressing, adding plenty of additional herbs if desired.

If you are serving them warm, stir the beans with 2 tablespoons of dressing in a saucepan and warm them gently before adding them to the potatoes, so that they absorb the flavoring. Otherwise, simply toss the cooked beans with 2 tablespoons of dressing and gently stir them into the dressed potatoes. Drizzle the remaining dressing over all, and serve either lukewarm or cold. A dash of garlic and additional chopped fresh herbs such as basil or parsley may be added.

Squash Casserole

There are many variations of this, and of course people are divided about the type of cheese to use. But most Southerners prefer plain old "rat cheese," the ordinary yellow cheddar that you can find in feed stores and hardware stores and the general stores in small towns.

2 pounds yellow squash, 5 or 6 individual gourds, sliced ½ inch thick
4 tablespoons butter
2 medium-size onions, sliced
1 garlic clove, finely chopped
1 cup milk
1 cup breadcrumbs
4 eggs, lightly beaten
1½ cups grated sharp cheddar or "rat" cheese
1 tablespoon salt
Freshly ground pepper

TOPPING:

4 tablespoons butter, melted
½ cup breadcrumbs

Preheat the oven to 350 degrees.

Grease a 2-quart casserole and set aside.

Put the sliced squash in a heavy pan and add enough water to cover. Bring to a boil, uncovered, then reduce heat and simmer for half an hour or until the squash is soft enough to mash. Drain, and mash with a wooden spoon, fork or potato masher.

Melt the butter in a separate pan, add the onion and garlic and cook until soft. Add this to the squash. Heat the milk in the same pan, stir in the breadcrumbs, and add this mixture to the onions and squash. Stir in the eggs, cheese, salt and pepper, and pour the combined mixture into the buttered casserole.

For the topping, combine the melted butter and additional ½ cup of breadcrumbs and sprinkle over the contents of the casserole. Bake for 30 minutes.

Green Beans and New Potatoes

Serves 6

This is one of those combinations that goes well with the Southern tradition of eating only vegetables at some meals. It's a recipe of Kate's, is good any time, and reheats well.

2½ pounds green beans, broken in
   1-inch pieces
¼ pound fatback
1 teaspoon salt
2 cups water
1 dozen small, new potatoes,
   scrubbed

Combine all the ingredients except the potatoes in a heavy Dutch oven. Bring to a boil and cover. Reduce heat to low and cook beans and fatback for 30 minutes. Add potatoes, cover, and cook for an additional 30 minutes. Remove lid and cook down until no liquid is left and the beans look brown—just a few minutes.

Candied Sweet Potatoes

Serves 4

These sweet and sticky potatoes are seen everywhere at Thanksgiving and for all kinds of important family dinner parties. They are good with ham, turkey or chicken.

4 medium-size sweet potatoes
1 cup sugar
½ cup butter
Water
½ teaspoon salt

Peel the potatoes and cut them into 2-inch slices. Put the slices in a wide, heavy skillet. Add water to a quarter of the way up the sides of the pan, cover, and cook slowly until they can be pierced with a fork. Remove from heat and drain the water from the pan. Sprinkle the sugar over the potatoes, add butter and salt, and return to low heat. Cook slowly, uncovered, until the liquid is sticky.

Collards and Turnip Greens

Serves 6

The greens of collards and turnips are cooked in exactly the same way. Collards taste a little like cabbage leaves. Turnip greens are more bitter, more like mustard greens in taste. Not all turnip greens have turnips —Shogoing turnips and seven-tops are among the varieties that produce no root. But there's little or no difference to report in the taste of the greens.

Spring and fall are the best times for turnip greens and collard greens. Some people cook the turnips, diced, along with the turnip greens. Since vinegar and hot sauce are always found on country tables, they are frequently used to douse the greens.

4 pounds turnip or collard greens
¼ pound fatback (salt pork)
1 tablespoon sugar
2 teaspoons salt or to taste

Pick over the greens to make sure that there are no worms or bugs. Fill the sink with cold water and wash the greens several times. Put the greens in a large pot of water and bring them to a boil; drain, discard the water and put them back in the pot with enough water to cover. Add the fatback and cook, covered, 2 to 3 hours; the longer they cook, the better they get. Add the sugar and salt to taste.

If you prefer, you may fry the salt pork and pour the fat over the greens after they are cooked.

Turnips and Red Peppers

Serves 4

Turnips grow easily here and are the perfect size for eating at about the time when green bell peppers turn red on the vine. If the turnips are larger than a tennis ball, they should be sliced, then blanched 5 to 10 minutes before cooking.

6 tablespoons butter
1 pound red bell peppers, sliced
1 pound small white turnips, peeled and sliced
1 large garlic clove, finely chopped
2 tablespoons red wine vinegar (optional)
1 teaspoon salt
Freshly ground black pepper

Melt 3 tablespoons of the butter in a large, heavy skillet or wok. Add the pepper strips, turnips, garlic and vinegar. Stir-fry over moderate heat, adding more butter if necessary, until the turnips are tender when pierced with a knife. Season with salt and pepper.

Turnip Gratinée

This dish was brought South by a Yankee friend and served at a wonderful dinner party. It is perfect for a Southern dinner, rich and unctuous, marrying well with ham or game.

1 garlic clove, peeled
1 tablespoon butter
1½ pounds turnips, peeled and cut in ⅛-inch slices
Salt and freshly ground pepper to taste
1 teaspoon dried herbs (parsley, tarragon, thyme, oregano), or 1 tablespoon fresh herbs, chopped
⅓ cup grated Gruyère cheese
⅓ cup grated Parmesan cheese
½ cup heavy cream
¼ cup fresh breadcrumbs
3 tablespoons butter

Preheat the oven to 400 degrees.

Rub a small gratin dish with the garlic clove, then butter it well.

Parboil the turnips for 2 to 3 minutes and drain. Arrange a third of the turnip slices in a layer in the dish. Sprinkle them with salt and pepper and half the herbs. Mix the 2 cheeses and sprinkle the turnips with a third of the mixture. Repeat layers, finishing with the cheese on top. Pour cream over the dish, sprinkle with the breadcrumbs and dot with butter. Bake for 45 minutes.

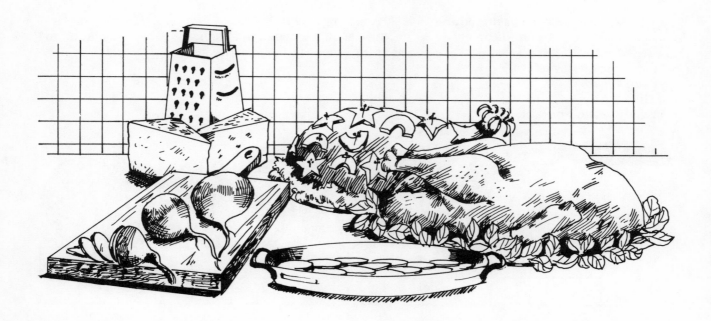

Pepper Jelly

Makes 4 pints

Many Southerners keep pepper sauce on their tables and put a dash of it on everything they eat. Pepper jelly is piquant but more refined, and is often seen, green- or red-colored, on top of cream cheese spread on crackers. It is also excellent with country ham, or on green beans or peas.

½ cup hot red pepper, seeded and coarsely chopped
½ cup hot green pepper, seeded and coarsely chopped
1 medium-size onion, quartered
1½ cups vinegar
5½ cups sugar
1 bottle liquid pectin

Place the peppers, onion and vinegar in a food processor. Process until very fine. Measure the sugar and pour it into a 6-quart pot. Add the pepper, onion and vinegar to the pot and let it come to a boil. Boil for 1 minute. Remove from stove and stir in pectin, skimming foam, for 5 minutes. Ladle into hot sterilized jars. Shake jars to keep peppers mixed. Let cool.

Stewed Tomato Conserve

Makes 1 quart

When tomatoes are plentiful, the Duprees put up this recipe in jars and keep them for winter days. The relish is excellent over green beans, blackeyed peas or butter beans.

2 pounds fresh tomatoes, skinned and quartered, or 2 1-pound cans of tomatoes with juice
½ cup cider vinegar
¼ cup sugar
Salt
Freshly ground pepper

Mix the ingredients in a heavy saucepan. Simmer until the mixture is thick enough to cling to a spoon. If you want to, add more sugar to make it sweeter.

Chow Chow

Makes 12 pints

Bountiful Southern gardens provide the foodstuffs for our relishes. This is just one of the many recipes with that name and different garden ingredients. It is, according to Elise, particularly good on ham sandwiches.

3 medium-size heads cabbage, finely chopped
12 hot red peppers, finely minced (less, if you prefer)
20 green tomatoes, chopped
12 green peppers, seeded and membranes removed, chopped
12 medium-size onions, finely chopped
½ cup coarse salt
2½ quarts white vinegar
5 cups sugar
2 tablespoons whole mixed pickling spice
4 tablespoons ground mustard
1 tablespoon ground ginger
3 tablespoons celery seed
1 tablespoon ground turmeric
4 tablespoons mustard seed

Combine all the chopped vegetables in a large kettle, and mix well. Sprinkle with salt and allow to stand overnight. The next day, drain off as much liquid as possible. Tie the pickling spices in a piece of cloth or cheesecloth.

Combine the vinegar, sugar, pickling spice bag and all other spices in a large kettle. Simmer 20 minutes. Add the vegetables to the mixture and cook over low heat until the mixture almost reaches boiling point. Pack the hot chow chow in hot sterilized jars and seal at once. Allow to stand 2 weeks before eating.

NOTE: The amount of red peppers may be decreased if a milder relish is desired.

MAIN COURSES AND GRAVIES

I well remember one time when a cousin of mine married a country boy from the Deep South, and started to find out what it would all mean. When she told me about it and things went from bad to worse, she was practically in tears as she exclaimed, "And he wants to have two and three meats cooked every night when he gets home!" Added to the four or five vegetables she was fixing nightly, the meal did seem an overwhelming task. But after a while you can get into the rhythm of it—some things are freshly cooked, others are reheated, or chicken-fried while you're cooking the stew for today as well as tomorrow. Pork is our traditional meat, chicken our traditional poultry, game is abundant. We like gravies—sauces, if you will—on our meats and breads as well as on our vegetables. I was quite astonished when I learned at the Cordon Bleu that gravies are supposed to go only on the meats. At home we thought they were supposed to go on everything on the table, and then be sopped up by buttered bread!

It's impossible to recount all the ways there are for frying chicken. And there are even more barbecue sauces than there are fried chicken recipes. It's only just lately that I sampled for the first time the mustard-based barbecue sauce typical of the Carolinas. In the South, each little town has its own way of doing things, and something that predominates, or perhaps even dominates. Lexington, North Carolina, for instance, has 19 barbecue places, and each one is more tantalizing than the next!

Beef Roast with Gravy

Serves 4

Beef wasn't originally used much in Southern cooking. When seen, it was usually served very well done—perhaps with the exception of rib roasts and fillets. Many times the beef was not "fed out," so it was not as tender as "store-bought" beef is nowadays. The vinegar was necessary to tenderize as well as to add flavor.

Some people add cooked sliced onions to the pan 45 minutes before making the gravy. Others add potatoes for the last 45 minutes of cooking.

1 beef roast (chuck, sirloin, or round)
¾-1 cup distilled or cider vinegar (¼ cup per pound of meat)
2-3 tablespoons flour
¼ cup water

Preheat the oven to 350 degrees.

Trim roast of unwanted fat and weigh. Place in a roasting pan with sides. Pour vinegar all over the roast in the pan. Place in the oven to sear. When the meat is brown, reduce the heat to 300 degrees. Place a loose tent of aluminum foil over the meat and cook approximately 20 minutes to the pound for rare, longer for well done. When the meat is cooked, remove it and place it on a hot platter to keep warm.

Mix the flour with the water in a small bowl. Remove any extra grease from the pan drippings. Add the flour and water to the pan, place over surface heat and bring to a quick boil, stirring briskly. Remove to a sauce boat. Slice the meat and pass the gravy at the table.

Country Fried Steak

This is one of those dishes for "meat and potato" men. Serve it with boiled, baked or mashed potatoes and green beans or turnip greens.

4 round steaks (¼ inch thick)
1 cup flour
Salt
Freshly ground pepper
1½-2 cups milk

Pound the steaks with the side of a heavy plate or a meat-tenderizing mallet. Mix the flour with a generous amount of salt and freshly ground pepper and sprinkle over both sides of the meat. Pound the flour in with the plate or mallet until the steak has absorbed as much flour as it can; avoid allowing the flour to become dry and flake off.

Heat ¼ inch of fat in an iron skillet. Cook the steaks quickly on both sides. Remove them from the pan and keep them warm. Add ¼ cup of flour to the pan and brown. Add milk and bring to a boil quickly, stirring. Pour over meat and serve warm.

Sirloin over Charcoal
Serves 4

Charcoaling is part of our way of life. Billy McKinnon, who is originally from Savannah, and has a Louisiana-style restaurant here in Atlanta, is a wonderful home cook. This is a recipe he says dates back to the Fifties, when the charcoal grill was first becoming popular.

2- to 2½-pound sirloin steak,
   2½ inches thick (preferably first
   cut off the butt and aged)
1-2 garlic cloves, crushed
Powdered sugar to taste
Butter to taste
Salt to taste

Rub the steak with crushed or pressed garlic about 1 hour before you cook it. Let the meat come to room temperature before grilling. Just before cooking, sprinkle powdered sugar liberally over the steak and rub with your fingers to a gooey consistency on both sides. The sugar will caramelize and seal the meat.

Place your prize piece of meat over white-hot charcoal that is at least 2 layers deep. Cook each side 1 minute, 1 inch above the coals, then raise the grill to 8 inches above and finish each side for 7, 10 or 15 minutes for rare, medium or well done.

To serve, slice the steak on the diagonal about 1 inch thick. Each guest should have his own serving of butter and salt so that he may top off each bit of steak with a soft piece of butter and a sprinkle of salt.

"Putting Up" the Whole Hog

Whole hog
Salt
Black pepper
Corn meal

At hog-killing time—around Thanksgiving, when the weather is real cold—kill the hog. Scald and get rid of the hair. Hang up by the heels and take the insides out. Put on a table and "block" it, that is, cut the hams and shoulders apart. Slit the backbone in half and remove the ribs. Pull out the tenderloins and have one fried sliced tenderloin for dinner with biscuits and gravy; save the other tenderloin for sausage. Lay out the rest of the hog overnight *to get cold* and trim it close, saving all fat and scraps to make lard and sausage. Salt the shoulders, ham, ribs, fatback (salt pork) and streak-of-lean bacon from the side (most people call it side pork); put it in a box for at least 6 weeks.

Then remove, wash the salt off and rub the meat with black pepper and corn meal. Wrap up and hang up in a cold place, preferably in a separate storehouse where the ground is dry and dug down some to make it cooler.

Cut the rind into cubes and render (cook over low heat a long time to make lard) in a black wash pot out in the yard. Strain up the fat in a lard can (this can still be bought from the country store).

Make sausage out of the lean scraps and some fat; grind up and season. Fry the sausage, put it in jars covered with fat to preserve, put lids on and turn the jars bottom-up. (They will last indefinitely on the shelf).

The hog's head can be used for Brunswick stew, pressed meat—head cheese or sausage meat—or it can be salted down to save and boil in the winter with dried peas.

All salted meat can be sliced and then fried. Usually salted meat is not cut until it is needed, as it lasts longer when in large pieces. Both sliced ham and baked ham can be salty and dry. When baking a whole ham it is advisable to check to see how salty it is by slicing off a piece first and testing it. Many times a ham should be scrubbed, then soaked for several days, changing the water frequently (if the water is not changed a brine is created, thereby resalting the ham) before baking. Do not soak a whole ham unless you are prepared to cook it when it has finished soaking. If you don't want the whole ham cooked, just soak the amount you need.

Country Ham with Red-Eye Gravy

Many people believe that salted "country" hams should never be baked, but sliced with a saw and fried. My favorite kind is salted, then sugar-cured. You can eat country ham uncooked as it is "cured" when properly salted; technically, it needs only to be heated through. Unfortunately, many people don't realize this and cook it until it's dry and hard. Experiment with one slice of the ham. If it is too salty, put it in water and rinse and change the water until the amount of salt is reduced to the way you like it. Saltiness of hams varies considerably.

TO SLICE AND STORE:

Lay ham flat, with side up that has the protruding line bone. Start slicing approximately ¼ inch thick at the butt end, slicing at the same 45-degree angle as the line bone. Do not slice straight across the butt end. You may slice the entire ham at one time. Once sliced, store in the refrigerator but do not freeze. If mold develops on ham in the refrigerator, scrape it off before frying. Layering foil between slices will help prevent the mold from forming.

TO FRY:

1-3 ¼-inch-thick ham slices

One of the following:
  3 ounces Coca-Cola or
  2 ounces water, 1 ounce black coffee or
  2 ounces water, 1 ounce red wine

Heat a 10-inch frying pan or skillet. Lay not more than 3 ham slices with the fat edge flat on the skillet bottom. Drape the lean portion over the rim of the skillet. Fry slowly until the fat edge is brown. Turn over and do the same to the other side of the fat edge. Now lay the whole slice on the bottom of the skillet and continue to cook on low heat until light brown. Turn each of the slices and cook the other side just until light brown. Do *not* cook until dry and hard. Put the slices on a warm platter.

Add Coke, or water and coffee, or water and red wine to the pan juices. Bring to a boil, stirring vigorously, then boil half a minute or until liquid has reduced almost to a glaze. Pour over the ham slices and serve.

Ham Steak in Mustard Cream

Serves 6

This dish using precooked packaged ham steak is good for a sophisticated Southern dinner party.

3 tablespoons butter
1 large precooked ham steak,
  2 inches thick (about 3 pounds)
2 tablespoons finely chopped
  shallots or green onions
2 tablespoons chopped fresh
  tarragon, or 1 tablespoon dried
1 tablespoon Dijon mustard
Salt
Freshly ground black pepper
2 tablespoons Madeira
1 cup heavy cream
2 tablespoons finely chopped
  fresh parsley

Preheat oven to 300 degrees.

Melt butter in a skillet until it sizzles. Add the ham and cook 3 to 4 minutes on each side. Remove the ham to a baking sheet and place it in the oven to keep warm.

Add the shallots, tarragon, mustard, salt and pepper to the butter in the pan. Add the Madeira and cream, stirring well. Cover over medium heat until the cream reduces and coats a metal spoon—about 5 to 7 minutes.

Carve the ham vertically into thin strips and arrange on a platter. Pour the sauce over and garnish with parsley.

Baked Pork Chops

Serves 4

Pork chops sold family-pack style are thinner than the regular size.

4 thick or 8 thin pork chops
Salt and freshly ground pepper to
  taste
2 tablespoons butter
½-1 cup flour
1 large onion, sliced
1 garlic clove, finely chopped
1-1½ cups water or canned beef
  broth
¼ cup vinegar

Preheat the oven to 375 degrees.

Season each chop liberally with salt and pepper. Melt the butter in a large skillet. Dip the chops in flour, add them to the hot fat and brown them on each side. Place in a baking dish. Cook the onion in a skillet until it is tender, adding more butter if necessary, and spread it over the chops. In the same skillet, brown 2 to 3 tablespoons flour, add garlic, water or stock, and vinegar, and stir until boiling. Pour over the chops and onions. Cover and bake 1 hour.

Barbecued Spareribs

Barbecues are tremendously popular throughout the United States, but the South lays claim to having originated this method of cooking spareribs.

4 pounds spareribs, cut in pieces of 5-6 ribs each
2 teaspoons salt
1 tablespoon vinegar
Barbecue sauce of your choice (see below)

Place the rib pieces in a large heavy Dutch oven. Cover with water. Add the salt and vinegar. Bring the water to a boil and cover. Reduce heat and simmer for 20 minutes. Drain immediately in a colander. Do not overcook. If you are not barbecuing immediately, spread the ribs on a platter to cool and to prevent additional cooking.

Prepare barbecue sauce.

Place the ribs on a hot grill or in the oven with the broiler on. Turn them every 5 minutes for 15 minutes, then start basting them with the sauce. Leave the ribs on the grill or under the broiler on each side until the sauce becomes sticky. Watch carefully or the sauce will burn.

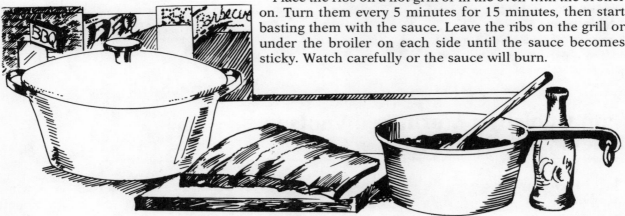

MARTHA'S BARBECUE SAUCE

Martha Summerour developed this sauce, which tastes "better than store-bought" and will last all summer in the refrigerator.

¾ cup catsup
2 tablespoons prepared (yellow) mustard
¼ cup cider vinegar
¼ cup molasses or dark brown sugar
2 teaspoons Worcestershire sauce
½ teaspoon salt
¼ teaspoon hot pepper sauce or to taste

Combine all the ingredients in a small saucepan and heat to blend the flavors.

Brush the sauce on the chicken pieces, halves of chicken, spareribs or backbone.

This is good for grilling outdoors, but do not start basting with the sauce until the meat is almost done. The catsup burns quickly.

COCA-COLA BARBECUE SAUCE

This adaptation from "A Taste of Georgia" is a thick, unctuous sauce that could be taken for the basis for a bottled sauce if you didn't know better. Good on chicken, ribs or any pork. (You know, the South is really not dependent on the Coca-Cola Company financially; it's just that without Coke a lot of us wouldn't know what to drink for breakfast.)

1 onion, chopped
2 tablespoons butter
2 cups catsup
1 small (10-ounce) Coca-Cola
1 bay leaf
1 tablespoon Worcestershire sauce
1 teaspoon mustard
2 teaspoons vinegar
2 garlic cloves, finely chopped
Salt and pepper to taste

In a medium-size saucepan, cook the onion in butter, add the other ingredients and simmer for 1 hour, stirring occasionally.

Sam Goolsby's Marinated Venison Fillets with Oyster Sauce

1 loin boneless venison or
   tenderloin
Bacon strips
4 garlic cloves, finely chopped
3 tablespoons soy sauce
1 cup vegetable oil
2 tablespoons red wine
½ bottle (2 ounces) oyster sauce

Cut loin into ¾- to 1-inch steaks. Wrap each steak with bacon and secure with toothpicks as you would a filet mignon. Combine the remaining ingredients in a bowl to make a marinade. Pour it over the meat and marinate 2 to 3 hours.

Pan fry the fillets in butter, or grill over hot hickory coals. Serve rare. Tougher cuts of venison can be cooked slowly until well done, as you would a tough piece of beef.

Country Captain

This is one of those dishes that is English in origin, but has been in the South so long that it's considered an old family recipe.

Meaty pieces of 2 frying chickens
½ cup flour
Salt and freshly ground pepper
½ teaspoon imported paprika
4 tablespoons butter
2 large onions, chopped
4 green peppers, chopped
1 garlic clove, finely chopped
2 teaspoons curry powder
1 teaspoon mace
2 1-pound cans tomatoes
½ cup currants or raisins
6 cups cooked rice
½ cup toasted blanched almonds
Chutney

Dredge the chicken pieces in flour that has been seasoned with the salt, pepper and paprika.

Heat the butter in a large skillet and brown the chicken pieces on all sides. Add more butter if necessary. Remove the chicken from the skillet and add the onions, peppers, garlic, curry powder and mace. Cook over medium heat until the onion is soft but not brown. Add the tomatoes with their liquid. Return the chicken to the skillet, skin side up. Cover the skillet and cook until tender, 20 to 30 minutes. Stir the currants into the sauce.

Serve over rice and sprinkle with toasted almonds. Pass the chutney separately.

Jean Sparks's Fried Chicken

There are hundreds of ways to fry chicken. Jean Sparks, who teaches cooking in Huntsville, Alabama, likes it pan-fried with a medium crust. For a thinner crust, dip the pieces only once in the flour. For a thicker crust, dip twice and don't knock off the excess.

2½-pound chicken, cut up into pieces
Vegetable shortening, approximately 2 cups
Salt and pepper
Flour

Wash the chicken pieces and put them in a colander to drain. Put the shortening in a 12-inch cast-iron skillet to melt. There should be enough to come halfway up the sides of the pan, and two-thirds of the way up the sides of the chicken when it is in the pan. While the fat is melting, salt and pepper the chicken liberally. Put the flour on wax paper or spread it on a baking sheet. Roll the still damp, seasoned chicken in the flour. Knock off the excess. When the grease is hot enough (just below smoking point, around 375 degrees), flour the chicken again and knock off the excess. Place the pieces skin side down in the pan. Pieces should be touching but not overlapping. Cover loosely. Reduce heat to medium high, and cook for 9 to 10 minutes, or until dark golden. Remove the cover, turn the chicken with tongs, and cook 8 to 10 minutes more uncovered. Drain on paper towels. Chicken should be dry and crisp, not greasy.

Cream Gravy

Gravy can be made from any pan drippings. In classic French and Continental cuisines, and in my mother's world of etiquette, only the meat is "sauced," covered with gravy. Not true in the South, where gravy goes on everything from biscuits and cornbread to mashed potatoes and even cold sliced tomatoes. It is made in the same iron skillet that the chicken or meat is fried in.

3 tablespoons of fat from meat or pan drippings
3-4 tablespoons flour
2 cups milk

Leave the fat in the skillet. Brown the flour in the fat a few minutes. Add milk and continue stirring over heat until it boils down and is thick.

Put it on the potatoes or tomatoes or biscuits or cornbread. Don't put it on crisp meat or chicken.

Blind Duck

As Conrad Zimmerman said to me, "The next time you go duck hunting, take a pocket knife, stick of butter, pepper and salt mixed in a little jar, a flask of brandy, good thick slices of rye bread, a small omelette pan, and a portable gas stove (prima or bluet). When you shoot your first duck, cut the skin as you would a jacket. Pull the skin back, exposing the raw meat. Cut a fillet the size of a hamburger off each breast. Melt the butter in the omelette pan. Pop a breast in, and cook a few minutes on each side. Slap between rye bread, and chase with brandy."

1 stick (8 tablespoons) butter
Pepper and salt, mixed
Duck breasts—mallard, pintail or
even Long Island

Melt the butter in the pan. Skin the duck and remove the breasts from bone. Cook the breasts 2 to 3 minutes on each side.

Willis's Fried Quail

There's a primitive excitement when hunters meet cooks. There are many ways to serve quail, but this is my favorite. Try this with the turnip gratinée, some turnip greens and apple pie.

2 chicken bouillon cubes
1 cup buttermilk
4 quail
1½ cups flour with 2 teaspoons
poultry seasoning
Peanut oil for frying

Dissolve the bouillon cubes in the buttermilk, then put the quail in to soak for 10 to 15 minutes. Remove the quail from the buttermilk and dredge in flour. Put enough peanut oil in a frying pan to come halfway up the quail, and heat to 360–375 degrees. Fry, turning once, until crisply brown and fork tender. Serve immediately.

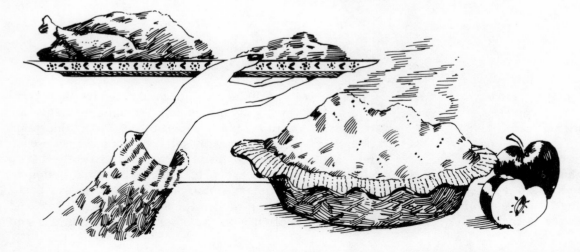

Game Birds

The way game birds are cooked is a matter of taste. I agree with the connoisseurs who think game birds can only be fully appreciated when rare or at least pink, cooked just enough to be a bit more than warm throughout. The French have a phrase, "flying through the heaven," to describe this just-warm temperature of cooking. This is particularly true of duck breasts, which compare to rare steaks. Larger fowl need to be moderately well done (it doesn't seem to me that there is much attractive about rare turkey or rare wild goose).

BASTING STOCK

Gizzard, neck and other spare parts
    from game birds (except liver)
1 carrot, sliced
1 onion, sliced
1 celery stalk
1 bay leaf
Freshly ground pepper

Place the giblets in a saucepan, cover with water, and add the vegetables and seasonings. Cover and simmer 30 to 40 minutes.

BIRDS

1 to 4 young game birds
    (depending on size)
½ cup butter or bacon fat
Salt
Freshly ground pepper
2-4 slices bacon
1-2 tablespoons flour for
    sprinkling
Watercress for garnish

Set the oven at the temperature indicated for the type of bird you are preparing (see chart). Wipe the insides of the birds with a damp cloth or paper towels. Put a tablespoon of butter or bacon fat with salt and pepper inside each bird and use string to truss them up and tie the bacon slices over the breasts. Heat the remaining butter or bacon fat in a roasting pan, put the birds in, and baste.

Roast in a preheated oven, turning the birds and basting them often with the stock so that the thighs and undersides are well browned. Cooking time varies according to the kind of birds you are doing (see chart). Test the birds by pricking the thickest parts of the thighs. The juice that runs out should be pink or clear, depending on how rare or well done you like your game.

Five minutes before serving, remove the bacon, baste the breasts well, and sprinkle them with flour. Baste again before returning to the oven for the final 5 minutes. This makes the skin brown and crisp. Remove the birds from the oven, discard the trussing strings, and keep them hot.

GRAVY FOR GAME BIRDS
1 teaspoon flour
½ cup well-flavored beef stock (optional)
½ to 1 cup stock from giblets

Pour off the fat from the roasting pan, leaving the sediment. Sprinkle in flour, and blend it into the pan juices. Cook 2 to 3 minutes or until the flour is brown, then pour in the strained stock mixed with beef stock, if you like, to improve the flavor. (You need 1 cup of stock in all.) Cook until the gravy boils, scraping the sides and bottom of the pan. Continue cooking 1 to 2 minutes or until the gravy is well reduced and well flavored. Season to taste, and strain. Garnish the birds with watercress and serve with gravy and game accompaniments.

COOKING TIMES AND TEMPERATURES FOR GAME
Cooking temperatures and per-pound cooking times for:
 Pheasant: 400 degrees, 30 to 35 minutes;
 Squab and pigeon: 350 degrees, 30 to 45 minutes;
 Dove: 425 degrees, 20 to 25 minutes;
 Wild duck: 400 degrees, 30 to 35 minutes;
 Quail: 450 degrees, 20 minutes.

Spicy Baked Shrimp

This shrimp dish worked its way up from New Orleans. It's typical of many recipes from Louisiana, Mississippi and the coastal regions of Georgia, North Carolina and South Carolina. You find it served in rustic restaurants or in homes with newspapers spread out to catch the mess. Shrimp should be cooked in the shell to intensify the shrimp flavor. The shrimp may be peeled before cooking or serving but they have more of the flavor of the sauce and less of the shrimp. This dish is good for an appetizer or a main course. Serve it with plenty of French bread to soak up the sauce.

16 tablespoons salted butter
1 cup oil
2 teaspoons finely chopped garlic
4 whole bay leaves, finely crushed
2 teaspoons crushed dried rosemary
½ teaspoon dried basil
½ teaspoon oregano
½ teaspoon salt
½ teaspoon cayenne pepper
1 tablespoon paprika
¾ teaspoon freshly ground pepper
1 teaspoon lemon juice
2 pounds whole fresh shrimp in the shell

Preheat the oven to 450 degrees.

Melt the butter in a saucepan, add the oil and mix well. Add all ingredients except the shrimp and cook over medium heat, stirring constantly, until the fat begins to boil. Reduce the heat to low and simmer for 7 to 8 minutes, stirring frequently. Remove the pan from the heat and let stand at room temperature, uncovered, for at least 30 minutes to infuse the flavors. Add the shrimp to the sauce, mix thoroughly, and return to heat. Cook over medium heat until the shrimp turn pink, 4 to 8 minutes, depending on size. Then put the pan in the oven and bake for 10 minutes.

For an entree, ladle the shrimp into 4 soup bowls, stirring the sauce to prevent separation. Use everything in the pan, even the solids that settle to the bottom. Eat with your hands, a soup spoon and plenty of paper napkins.

As an appetizer, drain before serving, and serve with a crusty New Orleans or French bread.

Trout Pecan

It's hard to tell if there are more fishermen or game hunters, both activities are so popular. Fresh trout is available nearly year-round from mountain streams or stocked ponds.

4 rainbow trout, cleaned and left whole
¼ cup flour, seasoned with ¼ teaspoon salt and pinch of pepper
3 tablespoons butter

SAUCE:
2-3 tablespoons butter
4 tablespoons chopped pecans
Juice of ½ lemon
Salt and freshly ground pepper to taste
1 tablespoon chopped parsley
1 teaspoon chopped fresh herbs, such as chives or thyme

Measure the thickness of each trout. Roll each whole fish in the seasoned flour. Heat a frying pan or skillet; when hot, add the butter. When the butter foams, add the fish and brown on both sides, turning once. Allow about 10 minutes per inch of the total thickness, half the time on each side. Do not worry if the butter browns. Do not add all the fish at one time because that reduces the heat in the pan and the fish will not cook as fast. If necessary, cook each fish individually. Place the cooked trout on a hot platter.

To make the sauce: Wipe the skillet or frying pan with paper towels, add the butter and pecans and cook slowly until the butter is nutbrown. Add the lemon juice, seasonings, parsley and other herbs to the pan at once, heating quickly, then pour the foaming butter sauce over the trout.

NOTE: For this dish use only fresh herbs; dried herbs will spoil the flavor.

Sarah's Scalloped Oysters

Serves 4

Marion Sullivan of Columbia, South Carolina, contributed this easy but authentic recipe for scalloped oysters. It comes from her mother-in-law.

1½ pints fresh oysters
2 cups large Saltine cracker crumbs
8 tablespoons melted butter
1 pint half-and-half
½ teaspoon salt
⅓ teaspoon Worcestershire sauce
Pepper

Preheat the oven to 350 degrees.

Drain the oysters and save the liquor. Butter a shallow baking dish (glass or china is preferred.) Pour the melted butter over the crumbs and toss lightly with a fork.

Spread a third of the crumbs on the bottom of the baking dish. Cover with half of the oysters and sprinkle with pepper.

Layer another third of the crumbs, the rest of the oysters; sprinkle with pepper.

Combine the reserved liquor from the oysters with enough half-and-half to make 1 cup. Stir in the salt and Worcestershire sauce. Pour over the oysters. Top with the remaining third of crumbs.

Bake for 30 minutes. Serve immediately.

SIDE DISHES

Side dishes are usually served in little flat bowls with sides just high enough to keep any liquid from spilling out. Each dish holds several heaping tablespoons of whatever is offered. Eggs are nearly a must in most side dishes, except for the ones that would be ruined by gravy spilling over from the meat. You would never put gravy on a side dish of macaroni and cheese, or rice custard, for example. You might put it on grits or rice, though—but never on sliced sweet potatoes, or on dripping-cooked potatoes, with their flavorful crunchiness.

Black-Eyed Peas

The black-eyed pea isn't really a pea at all; it's a bean. Be that as it may, black-eyed peas are served all year long, and with special emphasis on New Year's Day, for luck. Combined with an equal amount of cooked rice, they make a traditional dish called "Hopping John," and form a complete protein—a vital source of food for what Roosevelt called "the Shoeless South." The Jimmy Bentleys, who live in the oldest house in Atlanta—the only one that wasn't burned down in the war, I guess—combine politics and good food every New Year's Day with this recipe.

½ pound hog jowl
2 quarts water
1 pound black-eyed peas
Water to cover
Salt and pepper to taste

Boil the jowl for 1 hour to extract the juices and reduce the liquid. Remove the grease from the top, either by blotting with paper towel or by refrigerating to let the fat harden.

Meanwhile, put the peas in a heavy pot, with water to cover, and bring to a boil. Let sit 1½ hours, or even overnight. Pour off the water. Add the peas to the hog jowl broth, with or without the jowl. Simmer ½ hour or until tender but not mushy.

NOTE: For Hopping John, add an equal amount of cooked rice to the black-eyed peas and add some of the water from the black-eyed peas.

Dripping-Cooked Potatoes

You could serve this as a side dish, alongside others, for four to six people, but it will frequently be polished off by two—or even one.

½ cup bacon, sausage or meat
  drippings
4-6 medium-size potatoes, cut in large
  pieces or wedges
Salt and pepper to taste

Preheat the oven to 400 degrees.

Heat the fat in an ovenproof pan in the oven. When the drippings are sizzling hot, add the potatoes and return the pan to the oven. Turn the potato pieces occasionally to coat them all over in the hot fat, and leave them in the oven for 30 to 45 minutes, depending on the size of the potatoes. Drain when they are brown and crunchy, salt and pepper them, and serve immediately.

Sliced Fried Sweet Potatoes

Sweet potatoes are a truly American food. First cultivated by the Indians, they became a necessary staple for the early colonists. Usually they are surrounded by other very sweet things and are rarely enjoyed for their own flavor. Sweet potatoes fixed this way are delicious hot, but also wonderful when snuck out of the refrigerator in the middle of the night to be eaten cold.

¼-½ cup butter or shortening
1-2 large sweet potatoes

Melt enough butter or shortening over medium-high heat to cover the bottom of a ¼-inch-thick iron skillet.

Meanwhile, slice the potatoes *lengthwise*, in strips ¼ inch wide, resembling long schmoos. It doesn't matter if you leave the peels on; in fact, I prefer to. When the fat is hot, add the potatoes and cover the pan. Cook for 5 minutes, or until the slices lighten in color, and turn. The potatoes are done when they are tender but not mushy. Each slice should hold together when you turn it or remove it with a fork from the pan. Drain.

This dish may be made ahead and reheated quickly in hot fat. But remember that even a single large potato, when sliced, will fill the pan several times.

Baked Grits and Cheese Casserole

Serves 6

Grits are made of corn hominy. They are served in many homes with every meal, certainly with breakfast. This particular way of treating them is seen at covered-dish suppers, for events like Sunday School class parties or church socials. This dish can be made several days ahead and reheated.

6 cups water
1½ cups grits
3 eggs
2 teaspoons salt
1-2 garlic cloves, crushed
1 teaspoon paprika
Dash of Tabasco
1 pound sharp cheese, grated
1 stick butter

Preheat the oven to 350 degrees.

Butter a 2-quart casserole.

Bring water to a boil in a large saucepan; then stir the grits into the boiling water, stirring constantly until they are completely mixed. Cook, stirring, until thickened. Mix the eggs slightly and add a small amount of grits to the eggs, stirring constantly to prevent overcooking of the eggs, and add to the grits. Add seasonings, cheese and butter, mixing well. Pour the grits mixture into the buttered casserole. Bake for 45 minutes. Grits may be cooked in advance and reheated.

Macaroni and Cheese

Serves 6

Made from store-bought macaroni, this is still a special recipe. Try it with homemade pasta as I did once with fettucini and you'll never forget it. It is served as a main course, but can also be a side dish.

½ pound elbow macaroni or other pasta
8 tablespoons butter, divided
4 tablespoons flour
2 cups milk
Salt and freshly ground pepper
10 ounces sharp cheddar cheese, grated, divided
¾ cup breadcrumbs

Preheat the oven to 475 degrees.

Butter a 10- by - 6-inch baking dish.

Cook the macaroni in a large pot of boiling salted water until done (about 10 minutes). Drain.

While the macaroni is cooking, melt 3 tablespoons of the butter in a medium-sized heavy saucepan. Stir in the flour and blend well. Add the milk all at once, stirring until the mixture comes to a full boil. Add salt and pepper to taste and ½ cup of the grated cheese.

Layer the drained macaroni with the remaining cheese in the prepared baking dish, starting with the macaroni and finishing with a final layer of cheese. Pour the sauce over.

Heat the remaining butter in a small pan. Mix with ¾ cup breadcrumbs and sprinkle on top of the casserole. Bake for 6 to 8 minutes until browned.

Spoon Bread

Spoon bread is a typically Southern side dish. It is not really bread, yet it can serve instead of one.

1½ cups water-ground corn meal
1 teaspoon baking powder
1 teaspoon baking soda
1¼ teaspoon salt
2 eggs, beaten
3 cups buttermilk
2 tablespoons butter or margarine
¾ cup milk

Preheat the oven to 450 degrees.

Mix the corn meal, baking powder, baking soda and salt together in a bowl. Add the beaten eggs and buttermilk and stir. Drop the 2 tablespoons of butter into a 2-quart glass casserole dish, and place it in the oven to melt the butter and heat the dish. Swirl the butter to coat the dish and pour in the spoon bread mixture. Pour the milk over the top. Do not stir. Bake for 25 minutes or until the center is firm. Serve hot.

Rice Pudding

You'll see this dish in Savannah and all the other cities in the rice country, served as a side dish, and even sometimes as a main dish.

1 cup cooked rice
1 egg and 2 egg yolks, or 3 eggs
1 cup sweet milk
1 cup grated cheddar, "rat" or Swiss cheese
Salt and pepper to taste
2 tablespoons butter

Preheat the oven to 350 degrees. Combine all ingredients well, place in a buttered casserole dish and dot with butter. Bake for 30 minutes, or until the custard is firmly set. This dish reheats nicely.

BISCUITS AND BREADS

Faith Brunson is a friend and colleague who is the buyer for Rich's book department in Atlanta. Faith was born and raised in a little town in Mississippi, and she has lots of stories of what life was like down there when she was a girl. For one thing, she remembers that when she came home from school she would creep into the kitchen, stick her hand under the cloth covering the food on the table, and help herself to a nice cold biscuit. With one grubby finger she would poke a hole in it, and fill the hole with the dark sugar cane molasses that was made in those parts.

"You didn't need a plate," she explains. "You just took it right outside with you."

This childhood technique is not that far removed from that old pastry standby for children, "a purse with change." Using the roll recipe in this section, anyone can make such a purse. You just cut the dough into a round, brush it with butter and put little tiny balls of dough (that's the "change") in the center. Fold the dough over, press to seal, and after baking you have the treat that made generations of Southern children very happy.

By the way, in the old days it was not all unusual to have both hot bread and cornbread at every meal—and sometimes even *three* kinds of bread were offered.

Kate's Biscuits

Kate makes the world's most wonderful biscuits. She never measures her flour and prefers Southern flour (with a 9 or 10 percent gluten content) but says she can make them from anything. They are light and fluffy and moist.

2-2½ cups self-rising Southern flour
½ cup shortening
1 cup milk

Preheat the oven to 500 degrees.

Grease a baking sheet with shortening. Place the rack in the upper third of the oven. Put 2 cups of the flour in a bowl. Cut in the shortening with your hands or a pastry blender until the mixture resembles coarse meal. Add the milk all at once. Mix with your fingers or a fork until lightly mixed. Dough should be soft and very wet.

Rub your hands with flour to clean them. Keeping your hands dusted with flour, pinch off a ball of dough the size of an egg. Dip the ball back in the extra flour. Bring your ring finger and thumb together, and rotate the dough in the palm of the other hand to make a round ball of dough. Place on baking sheet and flatten slightly. Or form by rolling dough out ½ inch thick on a floured surface, cut into 3-inch circles with a floured biscuit cutter and place close together on a baking sheet. Bake 10 minutes until golden brown.

NOTES: To make crisper biscuits, roll them thinner and place farther apart on the baking sheet.

If the dough is rolled, more flour is needed and the biscuits will not be as moist.

If you don't want to heat up the oven, try the way a student of mine learned in Campfire days—melt butter in an iron skillet, add the biscuits while the skillet is barely warm; cover and cook on high 2 minutes, then reduce heat and cook on medium heat 3 to 4 more minutes or until brown. Turn, re-cover and cook 5 minutes more until done.

Beaten Biscuits

Beaten biscuits are a different kind of biscuit. They are firm, not light, more like a thick cracker. Bland, they are the perfect foil for salty country ham. I saw them made once by a Monroe, Georgia, friend who used a beaten-biscuit machine which looked like a washing machine wringer attached to a marble slab. The modern way is to use a food processor.

**6 cups Southern flour, sifted
  and measured**
1 teaspoon salt
1 tablespoon sugar
1 teaspoon baking powder
1 level cup cold lard or shortening
**½ cup cold milk mixed with
  ½ cup ice water**

Preheat the oven to 375 degrees.

Mix the dry ingredients. Cut in the lard with a pastry blender or fork or food processor until the lumps are out. Add cold milk and water. Mix with the hands or in a food processor, turning over in the bowl, kneading it in a mass. If dry or crumbly, add more milk. Either remove the dough from the bowl and place it on an unfloured cold surface such as a marble slab, or continue in the food processor. Beat the dough, popping blisters. Beat 1001 times with a rolling pin or heavy mallet, turning and folding from time to time, or 100 times through a roller, or knead it for 2 minutes in the processor. It should be smooth and marbled. Roll out the dough ½ inch thick. Cut in 1¼ inch rounds, ½ inch thick, and place on a baking sheet. Pierce with a fork, making 2 parallel sets of 4 holes in the center of the biscuit all the way to the pan. Keep rolling scraps and making more until there are 90 party-sized biscuits.

Place in the preheated oven and turn down to 350 degrees. Bake for 30 minutes. Do not brown. Serve, halved with a knife, hot or cold. They will keep for weeks in a tight tin or in the freezer.

Sally Lunn

Sally Lunn isn't really Southern at all. It originated in England and came to the Colonies. But scratch a Southerner and he'll tell you it's an old family recipe.

¼ cup warm water (115 degrees)
2 packages active dry yeast
1 cup milk
8 tablespoons butter
4 cups all-purpose flour, divided
⅓ cup sugar
2 teaspoons salt
3 eggs

Preheat the oven to 350 degrees 10 minutes before baking. Butter a 10-inch tube pan or bundt pan.

Dissolve the yeast in the warm water (about 5 to 8 minutes). Meanwhile heat the milk and butter together to 115 degrees. The butter does not have to melt. Place the milk mixture, the dissolved yeast, 2 cups of the flour, the sugar and salt into the large bowl of an electric mixer. Beat well for 2 minutes at medium speed. Add 1 more cup of flour and the eggs and beat on high for 2 minutes. Add the remaining flour and beat 1 more minute. The batter will be thick but not stiff.

Cover and let rise in a warm place at about 85 degrees until double (about 1 hour).

Beat the dough down with a spatula or on the lowest speed of an electric mixer and turn into the prepared pan.

Cover and put in a warm place and allow to double in bulk (about 30 minutes).

Bake for 40 to 50 minutes. Cool in the pan for 10 minutes, then turn out onto a wire rack to cool.

Sally Lunn may be served warm or at room temperature; it may be wrapped in foil and frozen.

Cornbread

Not only is this cornbread wonderful on its own but it is also wonderful dipped in "pot likker" (the liquid left from vegetables) or soups. It is equally good in a cereal bowl with milk poured over and eaten as a "comfort food" late at night, or even for lunch or supper. It may be sandwiched with butter and have peas or vegetables and their juices spooned over and then eaten with a fork.

3 tablespoons bacon drippings
1½ cups self-rising corn meal
½ cup self-rising flour
1 egg
1 cup milk

Preheat the oven to 500 degrees.

Place bacon drippings in a 9-inch skillet or a 9-inch-square pan and heat in the oven 3 to 5 minutes.

Mix the remaining ingredients in a small bowl with a fork or whisk.

Remove pan from oven and spoon half the drippings into the cornbread mixture. Pour into the hot pan and bake for 15 minutes. Cut into squares or wedges and serve.

Cornsticks

This variation on cornbread is firmer than the traditional kind, not quite as crumbly, and it is good for dipping in "pot likker" and soups. It's from Martha Summerour's collection.

⅔ cup cooking oil
1 cup self-rising corn meal
  (preferably stone ground)
1 cup buttermilk
1 egg
2 tablespoons oil

Preheat the oven to 500 degrees.

Put 1½ teaspoons of oil in each of the 8 sections of 2 cornstick pans, or 3 teaspoons in each of 8 large muffin tins. Use a pastry brush to coat each entire section with oil. Place the pans in the oven until they are very hot. Meanwhile combine the remaining ingredients in a mixing bowl. The batter will be runny. Remove the hot pans from the oven and fill each section half full with the cornmeal mixture. Bake the cornsticks for 20 minutes.

Hoe Cakes

Martha Summerour taught this recipe at our cooking school, bringing it from her repertoire of Southern cooking that comes down through generations of her family and their cooks. It may be served with any of the Southern vegetables. There are even those who like it without salt.

Vegetable shortening
1 cup corn meal
1 teaspoon salt
1 cup boiling water

Heat about ¼ inch of vegetable shortening in a heavy 9- or 10-inch skillet until it is almost smoking. While the oil is heating, mix the corn meal and salt in a bowl. Beat in the water with a spoon until you achieve a soupy consistency. Drop from the spoon into hot grease and fry until golden on bottom. Turn and fry on the other side. Drain on paper towels.

Hush Puppies

My memories of hush puppies are always of my wedding supper on the island of Ocracoke, North Carolina. They were served with freshly caught fish.

¾ cup self-rising corn meal
⅓ cup self-rising flour
1 large onion, finely chopped
1 egg
¾ cup buttermilk
Lard or vegetable shortening

Mix all the ingredients in a small bowl. Shape into flat rounds or into balls and fry in deep fat at 375 degrees until crisp and brown.

Sour Cream Coffee Cake

Makes 1 10-inch loaf

This sweet is for those times when neighbors and friends share a morning cup of coffee, gather for tea or visit after church on Wednesday nights.

6 tablespoons butter, softened
1 cup brown sugar, packed
2 teaspoons cinnamon
1 cup chopped walnuts
½ cup shortening
¾ cup sugar
1 teaspoon vanilla extract
3 eggs
2 cups sifted all-purpose flour
1 teaspoon baking powder
1 teaspoon baking soda
¼ teaspoon salt
1 cup sour cream

Preheat oven to 350 degrees.

Grease a 10-inch tube pan and line the bottom with greased wax paper.

Beat the butter, brown sugar and cinnamon together until soft and creamy. Add the nuts and mix well. Set aside.

Beat the shortening, sugar and vanilla together until creamy. Add eggs one at a time, beating well after each addition. Sift the dry ingredients together. Add to shortening mixture alternately with sour cream, blending well after each addition, to make a batter.

Spread half of the batter in the pan. Sprinkle half of the nut mixture evenly over the batter in the pan. Cover with the remaining batter. Sprinkle on the remaining nut mixture. Bake for 50 minutes or until done. Let cool 15 minutes before removing from pan.

Bailee's Sticky and Cinnamon Buns

Bailee Kronowitz is a new friend from Savannah. Her expansive, joyous way of looking at food—and teaching cooking—is infectious. She's generous in her cooking, and makes these buns larger than I do, so we've adapted her recipe a little.

DOUGH FOR BOTH:
2 tablespoons (2 packages) yeast
½ cup water
½ cup milk
4 tablespoons butter
4½ to 5½ cups unsifted
   all-purpose flour
½ cup sugar
1½ teaspoons salt
2 eggs

Dissolve the yeast in warm water at 115 degrees.

Combine the milk and butter in a saucepan, and put over low heat until the milk is warm.

In the large bowl of an electric mixer, thoroughly blend 2 cups of the flour, the sugar and the salt. Slowly add the milk mixture to the dry ingredients, and mix. Add the yeast mixture, and beat well. Add the eggs and a half cup or more of flour to make a thick batter. Beat at high speed for 2 minutes scraping the bowl occasionally. Add enough additional flour to make a soft dough. Turn out onto a floured surface and knead until smooth and elastic (about 8 to 10 minutes by hand) or continue to beat by machine for 3 to 5 minutes.

Place in a greased bowl, and turn the dough to grease the top. Cover with plastic wrap or a damp towel, and let rise in a warm place, free from drafts, until doubled—about 1 hour, or until an indentation made with your finger stays in. Punch the dough down; turn out onto a lightly floured board or countertop. Divide in half, and shape as desired.

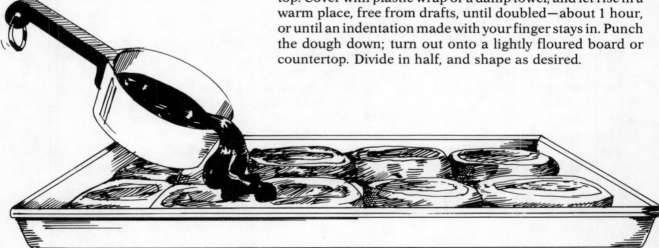

STICKY BUNS

½ recipe dough
8 tablespoons butter
⅔ cup firmly packed light
   brown sugar
2 teaspoons light corn syrup
¾ cup chopped pecans

FILLING:
4 tablespoons melted butter
¼ cup light brown sugar
1 teaspoon ground cinnamon

Preheat the oven to 400 degrees 15 minutes before baking.

While the dough is rising, prepare the pan with the sticky mixture: Melt the butter in a saucepan. Add the brown sugar and corn syrup, and bring to a rolling boil. Immediately pour into a 9-by-13-inch pan and spread before the mixture hardens. Sprinkle with pecans.

Roll out half the dough into a 12-inch square. Brush with melted butter. Combine the brown sugar and cinnamon. Sprinkle the center third of the dough with half the cinnamon mixture. Fold another third of dough over the center third. Sprinkle with the remaining cinnamon mixture. Fold over the remaining third of dough to make a 3-layer, 12-inch-long strip. Roll the strip to ¼-inch thickness. Cut into 1-inch pieces. Hold the end of each piece, and twist in opposite directions 2 or 3 times. Secure the ends together firmly by making a circle from the twisted rope and tuck under.

Place in the prepared pan, about ¼ inch to ½ inch apart. Cover and let rise in a warm place, free from drafts, until doubled in bulk—about 1 hour. Don't worry if the rolls touch each other when risen.

Bake 10 to 20 minutes, or until brown. After you remove them from the oven, invert the rolls onto a plate to cool immediately, so that the sticky part is on top. These are best served warm.

CINNAMON BUNS

½ recipe dough
4 tablespoons melted butter
¾ cup sugar, brown or granulated
⅓ cup seedless raisins
1 teaspoon ground cinnamon

Preheat the oven to 350 degrees 15 minutes before baking. Grease a 9-inch round cake pan.

Roll the dough into a 9-by-18-inch oblong. Brush with the melted butter. Combine sugar, raisins, and cinnamon. Sprinkle over the dough. Roll up as for jelly roll to make an 18-inch-long roll. Seal edges firmly. Cut each roll into 18 pieces about 1 inch wide. Place the rolls in a greased pan and don't worry if they touch each other. Cover, let rise in a warm place, free from drafts, until doubled in bulk—about 1 hour.

Bake for about 15 to 25 minutes, or until brown. Cool on wire racks, and don't break them apart into rolls until they are cool.

DESSERTS

Desserts are served religiously, at every Southern meal—we are the land of the universal sweet tooth. You don't see chocolates on our tables as much as you do fruit pies and light cakes, and pies and cakes for our wonderful nut, the pecan. In between meals and late at night, sweets-cravers creep to the "pie safe," which is a shelved cabinet with tin doors. Little holes are punched in the tin, and the idea is to keep the bugs out and the air in, to prevent mold and to keep the food and sweets fresher. In any good pie safe, you'll find pie and cake, and the ham might be kept in there too during the cooler months, if refrigeration is limited. The pie safe is surely the forerunner of the metal bread boxes and bins that were so popular in the Fifties. Today, alas, modernists refrigerate their bread, which simply makes it worse, and store only china in their pie safes.

Grace's Coconut Cake

Without coconut cake, many people wouldn't know what to have for dessert when the grandchildren come to spend some time. This is from a special grandmother, Grace Griffin of Scott, Georgia.

16 tablespoons butter, room temperature
2 cups sugar
4 eggs, at room temperature
3 cups cake flour, sifted before measuring
2 teaspoons baking powder
1 cup milk
½ teaspoon each vanilla and lemon flavoring
Coconut icing (see below)

Preheat the oven to 350 degrees.

Grease and flour 3 9-inch cake pans.

Cream the butter and sugar until light and fluffy. Add the eggs, one at a time, beating well after each addition. Sift together the flour and baking powder and add alternately with the milk, beginning and ending with flour. Stir in the flavoring.

Divide the batter evenly between pans. Bake for 25 minutes. Turn out on racks to cool before icing.

COCONUT ICING

2 cups sugar
1 cup liquid (1 cup coconut juice or ½ cup water and ½ cup milk)
6 tablespoons butter
1 grated coconut or 3 6-ounce packages frozen coconut
3 egg whites
1 teaspoon vanilla

Cook the sugar, liquid and butter until slightly thickened (5 or 6 minutes after coming to a boil). Cool thoroughly. Add the coconut after cooling. Beat the egg whites until they are very stiff. Mix thoroughly with the coconut mixture, return to heat and cook 3 to 4 minutes after it begins to "blurp" (don't cook over very high heat and be sure to stir frequently). Spread on a 3-layer cake while the icing is hot.

Pie Pastry

Although my favorite pie crust is made with a combination of butter and shortening, it is frequently too hot in the South to work with butter. Shortening is the most popular fat for sweet pies, but meat pies are made with lard crusts.

1½ cups flour
½ teaspoon salt
⅔ cup vegetable shortening or lard
3-4 tablespoons ice water

Put flour and salt in a medium-sized bowl. Using a fork or pastry blender, cut in the shortening until the dough forms in the size and shape of little peas.

Sprinkle the mixture with ice water and toss with a fork. A few drops more water may be necessary. The pastry is ready when it clings together when lightly squeezed with the hand.

If using a food processor, use the steel knife and short on-off clicks to bring the flour, salt and shortening to the little-pea stage. Add the ice water and process until the pastry begins to come into a mass. Stop processing before the mixture forms a ball.

Turn the pastry onto a lightly floured surface and form it into a flattened round. It may now be covered and chilled for 20 minutes or stored for several days in the refrigerator or frozen for future use. If frozen, thaw it overnight in the refrigerator.

Roll the pastry on a floured surface to ⅛-inch thickness. Roll it onto the rolling pin and transfer it to a pie plate, unrolling to place the pastry in the container. Trim the pastry, leaving a 1-inch overhang. Fold the loose edges under and flute the rim.

To prebake the shell: Prick the pastry all over with a fork. Cover it with wax paper, then fill with rice or beans to weight down the bottom and sides. Bake at 425 degrees for 10 to 12 minutes. If not to be prebaked, fill and bake according to recipe directions.

Ray's Lemon Meringue Pie

The trick for a nice meringue is to beat the egg whites by hand, in a copper bowl, if possible. The meringue should be spread over the filling while the filling is hot, and should be "sealed" to the outside of the crust to stop it from shrinking.

9-inch unbaked pie pastry shell
(see recipe opposite)
1¼ cups sugar
½ cup cornstarch
¼ teaspoon salt
1½ cups water
4 egg yolks
2 tablespoons butter
1 teaspoon finely grated lemon peel
½ cup lemon juice
4 egg whites
¼ teaspoon cream of tartar
½ teaspoon vanilla
½ cup sugar

Prepare and bake a 9-inch pie crust.

Combine the 1¼ cups of sugar, the cornstarch and salt in a medium-sized saucepan. Gradually stir in the water until the liquid and dry ingredients are well mixed. Cook and stir over medium-high heat until thickened and bubbly. Reduce heat; cook and stir 2 minutes more. Remove from heat.

Beat the egg yolks. Pour about 1 cup of the hot mixture into the yolks, stirring constantly. Return all of the egg yolk mixture to the saucepan. Cook and stir 2 minutes more to cook the eggs. Do not boil. The sauce should be very thick. Add the butter, lemon rind and lemon juice to the hot mixture. Mix well. Pour the hot filling into the cooled pastry shell.

Preheat the oven to 350 degrees.

To make the meringue: Beat the egg whites in an electric mixer with vanilla and cream of tartar until soft peaks form (about 1 minute). Gradually add the sugar, 1 tablespoon at a time, beating until the mixture forms stiff peaks (about 4 minutes with an electric mixer on high).

Spread the meringue over the hot lemon filling. Be sure to seal the meringue to the outside of the crust to prevent shrinkage. Bake for 12 to 15 minutes, until the meringue is golden brown. Cool before serving.

Pecan Pie

Pies are tremendously popular with Southerners. There's always some around when you walk into a country kitchen or home, for a snack or Sunday dinner. Pecan pie is particularly good with a cold glass of milk.

9-inch unbaked pie pastry shell
  (see recipe, page 74)
½ cup dark or light corn syrup
1 cup sugar
4 tablespoons butter, melted
3 eggs, well beaten
1 cup pecan halves

Preheat the oven to 400 degrees.

In a medium-sized mixing bowl, combine syrup, sugar and butter. Add eggs and pecans. Fill the unbaked pie shell with the mixture. Bake for 10 minutes. Reduce the heat to 350 degrees and continue baking for 30 to 35 minutes, until set around the edges. The pie will not be completely set in the middle when done. Cool before serving.

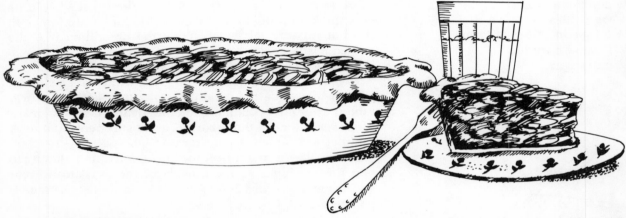

Lemon Chess Pie

1 cup boiling water
½ cup seedless raisins
4 tablespoons butter
¾ cup sugar
3 eggs
3 tablespoons fresh lemon juice
1 teaspoon vanilla
Finely grated peel of 1 lemon
9-inch pie shell, baked (see page 74)
1 egg white, lightly beaten

Preheat the oven to 350 degrees.

Pour boiling water over the raisins and let them stand about 30 minutes to plump them.

Meanwhile, cream the butter with the sugar. Add the eggs and beat well. Add the lemon juice, vanilla and peel and mix well. (Lemon juice will give the filling mixture a curdled appearance; don't worry, it will disappear in cooking.)

Position a rack in the lower third of the oven. Brush the pastry with egg white to waterproof the crust. Let dry 1 minute. Drain the raisins and stir them into the filling. Pour into pastry. Bake until the filling is firm and golden brown, about 45 minutes (if the pie begins to brown too much, reduce the oven temperature to 325 degrees). Serve at room temperature or refrigerate and serve chilled.

Fried Pies

Makes 14 pies

Fried pies may be made from a biscuit dough that has had more flour added, as below, or from a pie dough. They may be fried in a frying pan or in deep fat at 350 to 375 degrees. Kate trims her pastry with the edge of a plate.

8 ounces dried apples or peaches
½ cup water
⅓ cup sugar
Pastry (see below)

Put fruit and water in a medium-sized heavy saucepan and let stand for 1 hour or overnight. Cook over low heat until thick enough to cling to the spoon, about 45 minutes. Stir in sugar.

PASTRY
2 cups self-rising flour
¼ cup shortening
¾ cup milk

Place the flour in a small bowl. Cut in the shortening, using a pastry cutter or fork until the mixture is well combined. Stir in the milk to make a soft but not sticky dough that will roll out without sticking; add more flour to the dough if necessary.

Heat enough shortening in a heavy skillet to make ⅛ inch depth. Heat to medium hot. While skillet is heating, prepare the pies.

Pinch off a piece of pastry the size of a small egg. Place it on a well-floured surface and roll it into a 5-inch circle. Place about 2 tablespoons of apple mixture on the bottom half of the pastry round, leaving a half-inch edge uncovered. Fold top of pastry over apples, forming a half circle. Trim to within ¼ inch of the filling. Press the edges together with the tines of a fork. Prick the top of the pastry with a fork in several places. Place in a heated skillet and fry on both sides until golden brown. Serve hot.

Fruit Cobbler

This cobbler is seen in Southern-style family restaurants as well as in many homes. Kate and Grace both cook it regularly, using whatever fruit is in season.

8 tablespoons butter
1 cup self-rising flour
1 cup milk
1 cup sugar
2 cups sliced fresh peaches (or cooked apples, blackberries, blueberries, cherries)

Preheat the oven to 350 degrees.

While the oven is heating, place the butter in a 9-by-13-inch pan and put it in the oven to melt.

While the butter is melting, mix together the flour, milk and sugar in a medium-sized bowl.

Remove the pan from the oven and pour the mixture over the butter. Distribute the fruit and its juices evenly over the batter.

Return the pan to the oven and bake for 30 to 35 minutes until browned.

The cobbler may be served plain, or with whipped cream or vanilla ice cream.

Peach Butter

This is easy to make, and a food processor is a modern way of reducing the effort and the mess. Jars of peach butter make wonderful Christmas gifts.

3½ pounds ripe peaches
½ cup water
3 cups sugar, approximately
½ teaspoon cinnamon
½ teaspoon, scant, almond extract

Put the clean peaches in a heavy pot with the water. Cover and bring to a boil, reduce the heat and simmer for 20 minutes. Put aside to cool.

Lift the peaches out of the liquid, saving the liquid. Remove the peach skins and pits and discard. Puree the pulp and measure.

Return the puree and reserved liquid to the pot and add ½ cup of sugar for every cup of puree. Add the cinnamon and almond extract and return to the heat, uncovered. Cook over low heat for about 1½ to 2 hours until very thick, stirring occasionally. To test the thickness, spoon some peach butter into a cold saucer; no ring of liquid should separate from the edge. Taste for sweetness and add more sugar if needed, then simmer the butter for another 10 minutes.

Cool, then spoon into individual plastic containers and freeze, or keep refrigerated for several weeks, or place in hot sterilized jars and seal.

Meringues

Meringues are difficult to make in humid weather. In the South, therefore, the usual amount of sugar is not used, and a little light brown coloring is not regarded as undesirable. In fact, many of us prefer our meringues chewy and leave them that way.

8 egg whites, at room temperature
¼ teaspoon cream of tartar
1½ cups sugar

Preheat the oven to 200 degrees.

Cover a baking sheet with parchment paper.

Beat the egg whites with the cream of tartar until soft peaks form. Gradually add ¾ cup sugar, 1 tablespoon at a time, while beating. Beat until the meringue is very stiff, dull and no longer grainy. Gently fold in the remaining sugar.

For small baskets: Spoon or pipe the meringue mixture into 3-inch rounds on top of the parchment paper. Make a slight depression in the center of each round. Bake 1 to 3 hours. It is best if the meringues can remain in a turned-off oven overnight. When they are completely dry, meringues may be kept covered in a dry place, or frozen. If frozen, uncover to thaw and re-dry briefly in oven if necessary before using. Serve with peach butter or fresh strawberries and whipped cream.

Lace Cookies

Many families in small Southern towns have a tradition of inviting friends and family to come see their Christmas trees. The family table is laden with small cookies and sweets which are served with a punch, or maybe some eggnog with a "little something" in it.

1 cup sifted all-purpose flour
1 cup finely chopped pecans
½ cup light corn syrup
8 tablespoons butter
⅔ cup brown sugar, firmly packed

Preheat the oven to 350 degrees.

Blend the flour and chopped pecans. Combine the corn syrup, butter and brown sugar in a saucepan. Put it over moderate heat and bring to a boil, stirring constantly. Remove the pan from the heat. Add the flour and nut mixture gradually to the hot mixture. Cool slightly.

Drop the batter by level teaspoonfuls about 3 inches apart on a non-stick cookie sheet. Bake 5 to 6 minutes, or until most of the bubbling stops and the cookies are a caramel color. Remove them from oven and let them cool for a few minutes on the sheet until they can be handled.

While the cookies are still hot, remove each in turn and roll it into a cylinder around the handle of a wooden spoon. If they break, eat them. If they can be rescued but are too hard to be rolled, return them to the oven for a minute to soften them slightly.

Pecan Roulade

If rolling terrifies you, this may be baked in several layers and stacked like a layer cake, sandwiched with whipped cream.

6 eggs, separated
¾ cup sugar
¼ teaspoon cream of tartar, if using an electric mixer
1½ cups coarsely ground or finely chopped pecans
1 tablespoon baking powder

FILLING:
Confectioners' sugar for sprinkling wax paper
2 cups heavy cream
¼ cup confectioners' sugar
2 drops vanilla extract, rum or brandy flavoring
1 cup sliced fresh peaches, bananas or strawberries
Optional fruit: kiwi fruits, peeled and sliced

Preheat the oven to 350 degrees.

Oil a 10½-by-15½-inch jelly-roll pan and cover with oiled wax paper extending over the edges of the pan.

Beat the egg yolks and sugar with an electric mixer until they are thick and light. In a separate bowl, beat the egg whites until they hold a stiff peak. (If you are using an electric mixer, add the cream of tartar.) Add the ground pecans and of baking powder to the egg yolk mixture. With a rubber spatula, fold a large spoonful of the egg whites into the pecan/egg mixture, then fold this mixture into the egg whites. Do not overfold. Pour into the prepared pan. Bake for 20 minutes. The roulade will be puffy and light; it is done when it springs back when touched and when a toothpick inserted in the center comes out clean. Remove the roulade from the oven and cool to room temperature. When cool, cover with a slightly damp towel to make the top soft but not wet. It may now be refrigerated for several days.

To serve: Sprinkle a sheet of wax paper the length of the roulade with confectioners' sugar. Invert the roulade onto the paper. Peel off the wax paper backing in narrow strips. Whip the cream with flavorings and confectioners' sugar. Spread the roulade with the whipped cream and top with the sliced fruit; roll as you would a jelly-roll. Make a final roll to slide it from the wax paper onto the platter. Sprinkle with additional confectioners' sugar and decorate with whipped cream and fruit.

NOTE: The roulade may be frozen if peaches and/or strawberries are used as the fruit. Thaw it for several hours in the refrigerator and serve it while it is still almost icy in the center.

Pecan Cookies with Fresh Peaches and Cream

Makes 10 to 15 cookie sandwiches

This is a French recipe that has been adapted to include regional ingredients—in this case, peaches and pecans.

1¼ cups pecans
10 tablespoons butter
6 tablespoons sugar
1½ cups flour
¼ teaspoon salt
Confectioners' sugar (optional)

FILLING:

1-2 cups fresh peaches, or other fruit
   in season, sliced
1 cup heavy cream, whipped
1 teaspoon vanilla
2 teaspoons sugar
Additional whipped cream
   (optional)
Powdered sugar (optional)

Preheat the oven to 375 degrees.

Brown the nuts in the oven for 5 to 10 minutes, watching closely so they do not burn. Cool, and chop them in a grater or food processor until they are fine, but not a powder. Beat the butter and sugar together until it is creamy and white. Sift the flour with salt, add the nuts and stir into the creamed mixture to make a smooth dough. Divide into 3 equal pieces and shape into flat rounds. Place each between 2 sheets of wax paper and chill 30 minutes or until firm. Roll or pat out into ⅛-inch-thick rounds. Refrigerate if hard to handle. Remove the top layer of the paper, and cut into small 2- or 3-inch rounds with a cookie cutter. Remove to a cookie sheet. Bake 10 minutes or until the edges begin to brown. Be careful not to overbake. They will be soft when done and will harden as they cool. Remove them from the cookie sheets to racks to cool.

Store, covered, at room temperature or in the freezer. One hour before serving, whip the cream with vanilla and sugar. Sandwich the whipped cream and peaches between 2 cookie rounds. Immediately before serving, decorate the top with additional whipped cream or sprinkle with confectioners' sugar.

Pecan Tassies

A tassie is a small tart. It is easily frozen and is frequently seen at weddings and large parties. It is not as tacky-sweet as many pecan pies.

PASTRY:

3-ounce package cream cheese, softened
8 tablespoons butter, softened
1 cup sifted all-purpose flour

FILLING:

1 egg
¾ cup brown sugar
1 tablespoon butter, softened
1 teaspoon vanilla
Dash of salt
⅔ cup coarsely broken pecans

Preheat the oven to 325 degrees.

To make the pastry: Combine the butter and cream cheese in a small bowl. Stir in the flour. Cover and chill slightly. Shape into 24 1-inch balls. Place in tiny ungreased 1¾-inch muffin cups. Press dough against bottom and sides of cups.

To make the filling: Beat together the egg, sugar, butter, vanilla and salt until smooth. Place half the pecans in the pastry-lined cups; add the egg mixture and top with the remaining pecans.

Bake for 25 minutes or till filling is set. Cool; remove from pans.

Ambrosia

Serves 6 to 8

My friend Ginger Converse of Savannah says, "We generally serve Ambrosia at Thanksgiving and at Christmas, or any time when the oranges begin to look good and there are enough family and friends around to peel and section them. Ambrosia is a dessert it's hard to keep around long enough to serve. We find the best way is to hide it until dinnertime, and then serve it up with Grand Marnier or Amaretto sprinkled on top. It also makes a nice fruit salad made with fresh pineapple."

12 oranges, as juicy as possible
1 cup shredded coconut
Slices of 1 or more of the following: fresh pineapple, grapefruit, bananas or cherries, to taste
¼ cup Amaretto or Grand Marnier, or to taste

Peel and section the oranges carefully, saving the juice. Make sure that every scrap of membrane is removed from the oranges and any other citrus fruit you plan to use. Mix the oranges, juice and coconut in a bowl. Peel and slice any other fruit as required, and add to the mixture. Turn into an attractive glass bowl and sprinkle liqueur over just before serving.